Home Library

EDITOR: Maryanne Blacker
FOOD EDITOR: Pamela Clark

• • •

DESIGNERS: Louise McGeachie, Paula Wooller

• • •

ASSISTANT FOOD EDITORS:
Jan Castorina, Karen Green

ASSOCIATE FOOD EDITOR: Enid Morrison

CHIEF HOME ECONOMIST: Kathy Wharton

DEPUTY CHIEF HOME ECONOMIST:
Louise Patniotis

HOME ECONOMISTS: Tracey Kern, Quinton Kohler,
Jill Lange, Alexandra McCowan, Kathy McGarry,
Kathy Snowball, Dimitra Stais

EDITORIAL COORDINATOR: Elizabeth Hooper

KITCHEN ASSISTANT: Amy Wong

• • •

STYLISTS: Marie-Helene Clauzon, Rosemary de Santis,
Carolyn Fienberg, Jacqui Hing, Kathy Wharton

PHOTOGRAPHERS: Kevin Brown, Robert Clark,
Robert Taylor, Jon Waddy

• • •

HOME LIBRARY STAFF

ART DIRECTOR: Paula Wooller

ASSISTANT EDITOR: Beverley Hudec

DESIGNER: Robbylee Phelan

EDITORIAL COORDINATOR: Fiona Nicholas

• • •

PUBLISHER: Richard Walsh

DEPUTY PUBLISHER: Nick Chan

• • •

Produced by The Australian Women's Weekly Home Library
Typeset by ACP Colour Graphics Pty Ltd. Printed by Dai
Nippon Co Ltd in Japan.
Published by ACP Publishing, 54 Park Street, Sydney.

• • •

♦ U.S.A.: Distributed for Whitecap Books Ltd by
Graphic Arts Center Publishing, 3019 N.W. Yeon,
Portland, OR, 97210. Tel: 503-226-2402. Fax: 530-223-1410
♦ CANADA: Distributed in Canada
by Whitecap Books Ltd, 1086 West 3rd St, North Vancouver
B.C. V7P 3J6. Tel: 604-980-9852. Fax: 604-980-8197.

• • •

Pasta Cookbook.

Includes index.
ISBN 1-86396-012-0

• • •

© A C P Publishing 1993
ACN 053 273 546
This publication is copyright. No part of it may be reproduced
or transmitted in any form without the written permission of
the publishers.

• • •

COVER: From left: Lemony Seafood in Saffron Garlic Sauce,
Tomato, Anchovy and Artichoke Salad, page 45.
OPPOSITE: Double Mushroom Ravioli with
Burnt Butter, page 105.
INSIDE BACK COVER: From front: Apple and
Almond Custard Flan, Easy Peanut Honey Sauce with
Rice Noodles, page 113.
BACK COVER: Clockwise from front: Warm Beef and
Walnut Salad, Easy Beef Ravioli with Lemon Dressing,
Parsley Meatballs in Creamy Cheese Sauce, page 60.

PASTA COOKBOOK

Pasta and noodles fascinate us; their shapes are so varied and the number of ways to use them is almost endless! The name of the pasta, often Italian, describes its shape or type; for example, spaghetti means "little strings". Names often vary, so choose pasta by shape if you can't find what we specify. Where we specify fresh pasta dough, you can easily make this by following our step-by-step guide on pages 120-122. Filled pastas, such as ravioli and tortellini, are bought unless we specify how to make your own. The noodles we used are mostly of oriental origin. Also see the glossary for helpful information.

Pamela Clark

FOOD EDITOR

SOUPS & APPETIZERS

You will enjoy the fresh, light and pretty look of our marvelous appetizers, though some, of course, have to be classed as hearty eating! Some are hot, some cold, and some between, such as a warm pasta salad. There are lovely sauces, too, and soups, including our version of minestrone. If you prefer, serve these recipes as lunches, snacks or main meals. However, for good menu balance, the main course should not contain pasta if you serve it in a soup or appetizer.

SPINACH AND CABANOSSI PARCELS WITH PASTA

1 bunch (1¼lb) spinach
2 tablespoons olive oil
2 cloves garlic, minced
1 carrot, grated
2 small zucchini, grated
1 stick (¼lb) cabanossi,
**   finely chopped**
3 green onions, chopped
¼lb ricotta cheese
¼ teaspoon ground nutmeg
10oz fettuccine pasta

TOMATO SAUCE
2 x 14½oz cans tomatoes
2 onions, chopped
2 teaspoons dried oregano leaves
2 tablespoons tomato paste
2 teaspoons sugar

Add spinach to pan of boiling water, drain immediately, rinse under cold water; drain, press out as much water as possible.

Heat oil in pan, add garlic, carrot and zucchini, cook, stirring, until vegetables are soft; cool. Combine vegetable mixture, cabanossi, onions, cheese and nutmeg in bowl; mix well.

Place a rounded tablespoon of mixture on center of 2 overlapping spinach leaves, fold in sides and roll up firmly. Repeat with remaining mixture and spinach.
Just before serving, add pasta to large pan of boiling water, boil, uncovered, until just tender; drain. Place parcels in single layer in top half of steamer, cook over boiling water about 2 minutes or until heated through. Serve parcels with pasta and warm sauce.
Tomato Sauce: Combine undrained crushed tomatoes with remaining ingredients in pan. Bring to boil, boil, uncovered, about 10 minutes or until slightly thickened. Blend or process sauce for 10 seconds.

Makes about 20.

■ Parcels and sauce can be made a day ahead.
■ Storage: Covered, in refrigerator.
■ Freeze: Sauce suitable.
■ Microwave: Suitable.

SHRIMP AND NOODLE BUNDLES

12 (about 1lb) uncooked
**   jumbo shrimp**
7oz Japanese somen noodles
¾ cup cornstarch
2 teaspoons sake
2 egg yolks
2 tablespoons water, approximately
12 chives
oil for deep-frying

WASABI SOY SAUCE
2 tablespoons light soy sauce
2 teaspoons sake
2 teaspoons sugar
¼ teaspoon wasabi paste

Shell and devein shrimp, leaving tails intact. Break noodles in half.

Blend sifted cornstarch with sake, egg yolks and enough water to mix to a smooth batter. Dip each shrimp in batter, roll in noodles; cover, refrigerate 1 hour or until noodles cling to batter.

Add chives to pan of boiling water, drain immediately, rinse under cold water; drain.
Just before serving, deep-fry bundles in hot oil until lightly browned and cooked through; drain on absorbent paper. Tie each shrimp bundle with a chive; serve hot shrimp with sauce.
Wasabi Soy Sauce: Combine all ingredients in bowl, stir until sugar is dissolved.

Makes 12.

■ Shrimp and sauce can be prepared a day ahead.
■ Storage: Separately, covered, in refrigerator.
■ Freeze: Not suitable.
■ Microwave: Not suitable.

RIGHT: From front: Shrimp and Noodle Bundles, Spinach and Cabanossi Parcels with Pasta.

SPICY PUMPKIN SQUASH SOUP WITH BEEF TORTELLINI

½lb beef tortellini
2 tablespoons olive oil
1 onion, chopped
1 clove garlic, minced
½ teaspoon ground coriander
1 teaspoon ground cumin
1 teaspoon cracked black
   peppercorns
2lb pumpkin squash, chopped
1 potato, chopped
4 cups water
1 small chicken bouillon cube,
   crumbled
½ cup half-and-half
1 tablespoon chopped fresh chives
1 tablespoon chopped fresh basil

Add tortellini to large pan of boiling water, boil, uncovered, until just tender; drain.

Heat oil in pan, add onion, garlic, coriander and cumin, cook, stirring, until onion is soft. Stir in peppercorns, squash and potato, cook, stirring, for 2 minutes. Stir in water and bouillon cube, bring to boil, simmer, covered, for 15 minutes or until vegetables are soft; cool slightly. Blend or process soup mixture in batches until smooth.

Just before serving, return soup to pan, stir in half-and-half, herbs and tortellini, stir over heat until heated through.

Serves 6.

■ Can be prepared a day ahead.
■ Storage: Covered, in refrigerator.
■ Freeze: Not suitable.
■ Microwave: Tortellini suitable.

QUICK 'N' EASY CHICKEN SOUP

2 tablespoons (¼ stick) butter
¼ cup all-purpose flour
3 small chicken bouillon cubes,
   crumbled
3 cups hot water
½ cup crushed rice vermicelli
1 cup (7oz) finely chopped
   cooked chicken
2 tablespoons lemon juice
1 teaspoon dried tarragon leaves

Heat butter in pan, add flour, cook, stirring, until bubbling. Remove from heat, gradually stir in bouillon cubes and water. Stir over heat until mixture boils and thickens. Add vermicelli, chicken, juice and tarragon, stir until heated through.

Serves 4.

■ Soup can be made a day ahead.
■ Storage: Covered, in refrigerator.
■ Freeze: Suitable.
■ Microwave: Suitable.

LAMB SHANK AND CELERY SOUP

2 tablespoons olive oil
2 cloves garlic, minced
3 lamb shanks
6 cups water
1 cup dry red wine
1 tablespoon olive oil, extra
1 onion, chopped
1 cup (3½oz) pasta elbows
4 stalks celery, chopped
2 tablespoons chopped fresh parsley

Heat oil in large pan, add garlic and shanks, cook until shanks are well browned all over. Add water and wine, bring to boil, simmer, uncovered, about 1 hour or until lamb is tender.

Strain, reserve broth; remove lamb from bones, shred lamb finely. Heat extra oil in same pan, add onion, cook, stirring, until soft. Add reserved broth, bring to boil, add pasta, boil, uncovered, until pasta is almost tender. Stir in celery and lamb, simmer further 10 minutes. Add parsley just before serving.

Serves 6.

■ Soup can be made a day ahead.
■ Storage: Covered, in refrigerator.
■ Freeze: Suitable.
■ Microwave: Suitable.

LEFT: Clockwise from top: Spicy Pumpkin Squash Soup with Beef Tortellini, Lamb Shank and Celery Soup, Quick 'n' Easy Chicken Soup.

CHILI WONTON SOUP

1 carrot
6 cups water
2 stalks celery, chopped
2 small beef bouillon cubes, crumbled
½ teaspoon grated fresh gingerroot
3 green onions, chopped

WONTONS

2 tablespoons (¼ stick) butter
1 onion, finely chopped
2 teaspoons all-purpose flour
¼lb ground pork and veal
2 mushrooms, finely chopped
1 tablespoon tomato paste
1 teaspoon Worcestershire sauce
¼ teaspoon chili powder
36 x 3½in square wonton skins

Cut carrot into thin strips. Combine carrot, water, celery, bouillon cubes, gingerroot and onions in pan, bring to boil, boil, uncovered, for 5 minutes. Add wontons, cook 1 minute before serving.

Wontons: Heat butter in pan, add onion, cook, stirring, until soft. Combine onion, flour, pork and veal, mushrooms, paste, sauce and chili in bowl; mix well.

Place 1 heaped teaspoon of mixture on center of each wonton skin. Brush edges of skins lightly with water, gather edges

around filling, pinch together firmly.

Add wontons to pan of boiling water, boil, uncovered, until wontons float to surface, simmer 10 minutes; drain.

Makes 36.

- ■ Wontons can be prepared a day ahead. Soup base can be made a day ahead.
- ■ Storage: Covered, in refrigerator.
- ■ Freeze: Uncooked wontons suitable.
- ■ Microwave: Soup base suitable.

SHRIMP AND NOODLE SALAD WITH HONEY DRESSING

½lb fine fresh egg noodles
2 stalks celery, chopped
1 large carrot, chopped
1 large onion, chopped
¼lb snow peas
1lb cooked shrimp, shelled, deveined

HONEY DRESSING
½ cup light soy sauce
½ cup water
3 tablespoons honey
3 tablespoons chopped fresh cilantro
1 clove garlic, minced

Add noodles to large pan of boiling water, boil, uncovered, until just tender, drain; rinse under cold water, drain.

Cut noodles in half. Boil, steam or microwave vegetables until just tender, rinse under cold water, drain.
Just before serving, combine noodles, vegetables and shrimp in bowl; top with honey dressing.
Honey Dressing: Combine all ingredients in jar; shake well.

Serves 6.

- ■ Can be prepared a day ahead.
- ■ Storage: Covered, in refrigerator.
- ■ Freeze: Not suitable.
- ■ Microwave: Suitable.

CREAMED MUSHROOM AND PASTRAMI PASTA

1lb pasta twists
1 tablespoon butter
1 tablespoon olive oil
2 cloves garlic, minced
4 green onions, sliced
1 small red bell pepper, sliced
7oz button mushrooms, halved
1 small chicken bouillon cube, crumbled
2 teaspoons cornstarch
1 cup water
½ cup dry white wine
¼ teaspoon dried marjoram leaves
¼lb sliced pastrami
½ cup heavy cream

Add pasta to large pan of boiling water, boil, uncovered, until just tender; drain.

Heat butter and oil in pan, add garlic, cook, stirring, 1 minute. Add onions, pepper and mushrooms, stir over heat for 2 minutes. Blend bouillon cube and cornstarch with 3 tablespoons of the water in bowl, stir in remaining water, wine and

marjoram. Stir cornstarch mixture into vegetable mixture, stir until sauce boils and thickens. Cut pastrami into strips.
Just before serving, combine warm sauce, pastrami, cream and noodles in pan, stir until heated through.

Serves 4.

- ■ Can be prepared 6 hours ahead.
- ■ Storage: Covered, at room temperature.
- ■ Freeze: Not suitable.
- ■ Microwave: Suitable.

LEFT: Clockwise from left: Chili Wonton Soup, Creamed Mushroom and Pastrami Pasta, Shrimp and Noodle Salad with Honey Dressing.
ABOVE: Angel Pasta with Creamy Salmon and Caviar.

ANGEL PASTA WITH CREAMY SALMON AND CAVIAR

½lb angels' hair pasta
3½oz smoked salmon pieces
1¼ cups heavy cream
3 tablespoons chopped red onion
2 tablespoons chopped fresh chives
1½oz salmon roe (caviar)

Add pasta to large pan of boiling water, boil, uncovered, until just tender, drain; keep warm.

Cut salmon into strips. Heat cream in pan, bring to boil, simmer, add onion, cook until heated through. Stir in chives, remove from heat, add salmon and roe. Stir gently to separate roe. Serve sauce over pasta.

Serves 4.

- ■ Best made close to serving.
- ■ Freeze: Not suitable.
- ■ Microwave: Pasta suitable.

SESAME ROAST DUCK WITH HERBED PASTA

1 quantity herbed pasta dough
1 Chinese roast duck
11oz can mandarin orange
   segments, drained
3oz snow pea sprouts

SESAME DRESSING
⅓ cup olive oil
1 tablespoon Oriental sesame oil
¼ teaspoon five-spice powder
1 clove garlic, minced
⅓ cup lime juice
2 tablespoons honey
1 teaspoon sesame seeds

Roll dough until ⅛ inch thick, cut into 8 x 5 inch squares. Add pasta to large pan of boiling water, boil, uncovered, until just tender, drain, rinse under hot water; drain.

Remove meat from duck, cut meat into ½ inch slices. Combine duck meat, mandarin segments and sprouts in bowl.

Just before serving, place a square of pasta onto each plate. Divide half the duck mixture over squares, sprinkle with a little of the dressing; repeat layering.

Sesame Dressing: Combine all ingredients in jar; shake well.

Serves 4.

■ Can be prepared 6 hours ahead.
■ Storage: Covered, in refrigerator.
■ Freeze: Not suitable.
■ Microwave: Pasta suitable.

BELOW: Sesame Roast Duck with Herbed Pasta.
RIGHT: From left: Chicken Wing Pockets with Tasty Orzo Filling, Minestrone.

MINESTRONE

3 tablespoons olive oil
2lb veal bones
12 cups water
4 ripe tomatoes, peeled, chopped
1½ cups (7oz) small macaroni pasta
2 carrots, chopped
1 leek, thinly sliced
2 zucchini, sliced
16oz can red kidney beans,
   rinsed, drained
3 tablespoons tomato paste
½ teaspoon sugar
3 spinach leaves, shredded
¼ cup chopped fresh parsley

Heat oil in large heavy-based saucepan, add bones, cook, stirring, until well browned all over. Add water, bring to boil, simmer, covered, for 1 hour. Remove and discard bones from broth.

Bring broth to boil, stir in tomatoes and macaroni, simmer, uncovered, for 10 minutes. Stir in carrots, leek, zucchini, beans, paste and sugar. Bring to boil, simmer, uncovered, about 10 minutes or until leek is tender. Stir in spinach and parsley just before serving.

Serves 8.

■ Recipe can be made a day ahead.
■ Storage: Covered, in refrigerator.
■ Freeze: Not suitable.
■ Microwave: Not suitable.

CHICKEN WING POCKETS WITH TASTY ORZO FILLING

8 large chicken wings
⅓ cup orzo pasta
3 tablespoons chopped fresh basil
1 tablespoon chopped fresh chives
2oz chopped salami
**3 tablespoons chopped pitted
   black olives**
**½ teaspoon cracked black
   peppercorns**
2 tablespoons tomato paste
1 teaspoon olive oil
2 tablespoons (¼ stick) butter, melted
**⅓ cup grated fresh
   Parmesan cheese**

Holding large end of third joint of chicken wing, trim around bone with knife. Cut, scrape and push chicken meat down to second joint, without cutting through skin.

Twist bone and remove; discard bone.

Add pasta to large pan of boiling water, boil, uncovered, until just tender; drain. Combine pasta, herbs, salami, olives, peppercorns, paste and oil in bowl. Spoon mixture into chicken wing cavities, secure openings with toothpicks.

Just before serving, brush wings with butter, place on wire rack over roasting pan. Bake in a 350°F oven for 30 minutes, sprinkle with cheese, bake further 10 minutes or until chicken is cooked through.

Makes 8.

■ Can be prepared a day ahead.
■ Storage: Covered, in refrigerator.
■ Freeze: Uncooked wings suitable.
■ Microwave: Pasta suitable.

SCALLOP RAVIOLI WITH LOBSTER BASIL SAUCE

1 quantity plain pasta dough

SCALLOP FILLING
10oz sea scallops
1 egg white
3 tablespoons grated Parmesan cheese
¼ cup heavy cream

LOBSTER BASIL SAUCE
1 medium lobster tail
2 tablespoons (¼ stick) butter
1 onion, finely chopped
1 clove garlic, minced
1¼ cups heavy cream
¼ cup dry white wine
1½ teaspoons cornstarch
1 tablespoon water
3 tablespoons shredded fresh basil leaves

Roll pasta dough until ⅛ inch thick, cut into 24 x 3½ inch rounds. Spoon filling evenly onto centers of half the rounds, leaving a ¼ inch border around edges. Brush edges lightly with water, top with remaining rounds, pinch edges firmly together to seal.

Just before serving, add ravioli to large pan of boiling water, boil, uncovered, about 3 minutes or until tender; drain. Serve ravioli with sauce.

Scallop Filling: Blend or process scallops, egg white and cheese until smooth. Add cream, process until just combined.

Lobster Basil Sauce: Remove meat from lobster tail, chop meat finely. Heat butter in pan, add onion and garlic, cook, stirring, until onion is soft. Add meat, cook,

stirring, for 1 minute. Stir in cream and wine, then blended cornstarch and water, stir over heat until sauce boils and thickens; stir in basil.

Serves 4 to 6.

■ Ravioli and sauce can be made a day ahead.
■ Storage: Covered, in refrigerator.
■ Freeze: Uncooked ravioli suitable.
■ Microwave: Not suitable.

HERBED BEEF PARCELS WITH RED BELL PEPPER SAUCE

¼ quantity plain pasta dough
1 tablespoon olive oil
1 small onion, chopped
2 cloves garlic, minced
1 lb ground beef
⅓ cup dry red wine
½ cup sour cream
¼ cup grated gruyere cheese
2 tablespoons chopped
    fresh parsley
2 tablespoons chopped fresh basil
2 tablespoons chopped
    fresh chives
1 tablespoon tomato paste
1 small beef bouillon cube, crumbled
1 tablespoon sour cream, extra
1 tablespoon heavy cream
2 teaspoons chopped fresh
    chives, extra
3 tablespoons grated gruyere
    cheese, extra

RED BELL PEPPER SAUCE
2 red bell peppers
14½oz can tomatoes
¼ cup heavy cream
¼ teaspoon sugar

Roll pasta dough until ⅛ inch thick, cut into 4 x 5 inch squares. Add squares to large pan of boiling water, boil, uncovered, until just tender; drain.

Heat oil in pan, add onion and garlic, cook, stirring, until onion is soft. Add beef, cook, stirring, until well browned. Stir in wine, sour cream, cheese, herbs, paste and bouillon cube. Bring to boil, simmer, uncovered, about 10 minutes or until thickened.

Place quarter of the meat mixture on center of each pasta square, pinch corners together. Spoon sauce onto plates, pipe with combined extra sour cream and heavy cream, top with parcel, then extra chives and extra cheese.

Red Bell Pepper Sauce: Quarter peppers, remove seeds and membrane. Broil peppers, skin-side-up, until skin blackens and blisters; peel skin. Blend or process peppers, undrained tomatoes, cream and sugar until smooth.

Serves 4.

■ Recipe best made just before serving.
■ Freeze: Not suitable.
■ Microwave: Pasta suitable.

CHEESE TORTELLINI LOAF WITH TOMATO SALSA

1 lb cheese tortellini
4 eggs, lightly beaten
1¼ cups half-and-half
1 cup (2½oz) grated fresh
    Parmesan cheese

TOMATO SALSA
3 ripe tomatoes, peeled, chopped
4 green onions, chopped
2 tablespoons chopped fresh basil
½ teaspoon sugar

Lightly grease 5½ inch x 8½ inch loaf pan, line base with paper, grease paper. Add tortellini to large pan of boiling water, boil, uncovered, until tortellini is just tender; drain.

Combine eggs, half-and-half and cheese in bowl, beat until just combined. Stir in tortellini, pour mixture into prepared pan. Place pan in roasting pan, pour enough boiling water into roasting pan to come halfway up sides of loaf pan. Bake, uncovered, in 350°F oven about 45 minutes or until set. Serve warm loaf, cut into slices, with tomato salsa.

Tomato Salsa: Combine all ingredients in bowl; mix well.

Serves 6.

■ Recipe can be made a day ahead.
■ Storage: Covered, in refrigerator.
■ Freeze: Not suitable.
■ Microwave: Tortellini suitable.

LEFT: From left: Herbed Beef Parcels with Red Bell Pepper Sauce, Scallop Ravioli with Lobster Basil Sauce.
ABOVE: Cheese Tortellini Loaf with Tomato Salsa.

NUTTY CHICKEN AND PASTA LOAF WITH EGG SURPRISES

½ cup orzo pasta
1¼lb chicken thighs, boned, skinned
1 clove garlic, minced
1 onion, chopped
3 tablespoons tomato paste
1 teaspoon dried marjoram leaves
1 small chicken bouillon cube, crumbled
1 zucchini, finely chopped
⅓ cup pine nuts, toasted
4 hard-boiled eggs
½ bunch (10oz) spinach

CHUTNEY MAYONNAISE
½ cup mayonnaise
¼ cup half-and-half
¼ cup mango chutney
2 tablespoons chopped fresh mint

Line base and sides of 4½ inch x 8½ inch ovenproof loaf dish with plastic wrap. Add pasta to pan of boiling water, boil, uncovered, until just tender; drain, cool.

Blend or process chicken, garlic, onion, paste, marjoram and bouillon cube until smooth; transfer mixture to bowl. Combine chicken mixture with pasta, zucchini, nuts and 1 chopped egg; mix well.

Add spinach to pan of boiling water, drain immediately, rinse under cold water; drain, pat dry with absorbent paper.

Line base and sides of prepared dish with three-quarters of the spinach leaves. Press half the chicken mixture evenly over base of dish, place remaining eggs along center, cover with remaining chicken mixture, pressing down firmly, smooth surface. Top with remaining spinach. Cover dish with plastic wrap, then foil.

Place dish in roasting pan, pour in enough boiling water to come halfway up sides of dish. Bake in 350°F oven for 1 hour. Stand loaf 5 minutes before turning out. Serve loaf warm or cold with chutney mayonnaise.

Chutney Mayonnaise: Blend or process mayonnaise, half-and-half and chutney until smooth; stir in mint.

Serves 6.

■ Recipe can be prepared or made a day ahead.
■ Storage: Covered, in refrigerator.
■ Freeze: Not suitable.
■ Microwave: Pasta and spinach suitable.

SALAD OF PASTA PILLOWS WITH BALSAMIC VINAIGRETTE

1 quantity plain pasta dough
1 bunch chicory
1 red leaf lettuce
½lb cherry tomatoes

TURKEY AND NUT FILLING
2 teaspoons olive oil
1 small onion, chopped
¼ bunch (5oz) spinach, chopped
10oz sliced turkey breast roll, chopped
⅓ cup pine nuts, toasted
1 tablespoon grated Parmesan cheese
2 tablespoons cottage cheese

BALSAMIC VINAIGRETTE
½ cup olive oil
3 tablespoons balsamic vinegar
2 teaspoons lemon juice
1 clove garlic, minced
2 teaspoons chopped fresh basil

Roll pasta dough until ⅛ inch thick, cut 2½ inch rounds from pasta. Top each round with 1 level teaspoon of filling, brush edges lightly with water, fold rounds in half, press edges together firmly.

Just before serving, add pasta pillows to large pan of boiling water, boil, uncovered, about 4 minutes or until tender; drain well, cool.

Place chicory, lettuce, pasta pillows and tomatoes on plate, pour over vinaigrette.

Turkey and Nut Filling: Heat oil in pan, add onion, cook, stirring, until soft. Blend or process spinach until fine, add onion mixture, turkey, nuts and cheeses, blend or process until fine.

Balsamic Vinaigrette: Combine all ingredients in jar; shake well.

Serves 6.

■ Pasta pillows can be prepared 6 hours ahead. Vinaigrette can be made 2 days ahead.
■ Storage: Covered, in refrigerator.
■ Freeze: Uncooked pasta pillows suitable.
■ Microwave: Not suitable.

HERBED FISH AND PASTA SOUP

1 tablespoon butter
1 leek, thinly sliced
1 carrot, chopped
1 teaspoon chopped fresh thyme
10oz white fish fillets, chopped
3½oz angels' hair pasta

FISH BROTH
1lb fish bones
6 cups water

Heat butter in pan, add leek and carrot, cook, stirring, until leek is soft. Add thyme and 5 cups of the fish broth, bring to boil, simmer, uncovered, about 15 minutes or until carrot is soft. Add fish and pasta, bring to boil, boil, uncovered, about 10 minutes or until pasta is tender.

Fish Broth: Combine fish bones and water in large pan, Bring to boil, simmer, uncovered, for 20 minutes; strain.

Serves 4.
■ Soup can be made a day ahead.
■ Storage: Covered, in refrigerator.
■ Freeze: Fish broth suitable.
■ Microwave: Soup suitable.

ABOVE: From left: Nutty Chicken and Pasta Loaf with Egg Surprises, Herbed Fish and Pasta Soup, Salad of Pasta Pillows with Balsamic Vinaigrette.

STEAK STRIPS WITH TOMATO TAGLIATELLE

¾lb piece rump steak
7oz broccoli, chopped
3 tablespoons chopped
    fresh cilantro
2 tablespoons chopped fresh parsley
1 clove garlic, minced
12 thick slices bread
2 tablespoons (¼ stick) butter, melted
1 tablespoon olive oil
¾lb tomato tagliatelle pasta
2 tablespoons olive oil, extra
1 onion, thinly sliced

FRUITY YOGURT SAUCE
1 egg
2 tablespoons chutney
1 teaspoon grated lemon zest
3 tablespoons lemon juice
¼ cup plain yogurt
2 tablespoons finely chopped
    fresh mint

Cut excess fat from steak, cut steak into thin strips. Combine steak, broccoli, herbs and garlic in bowl, mix well; cover mixture, refrigerate 1 hour.

Cut a 3 inch round from each slice of bread, brush both sides of rounds with combined butter and oil. Place rounds onto baking sheet, bake in 350°F oven about 15 minutes or until well browned.

Just before serving, add pasta to large pan of boiling water, boil, uncovered, until just tender; drain.

Heat extra oil in pan, add onion, cook, stirring, until lightly browned. Add steak mixture, cook, stirring, until steak is well browned and tender. Combine steak mixture with pasta, serve on warm toast rounds with sauce.

Fruity Yogurt Sauce: Blend or process all ingredients until smooth.

Serves 6.

■ Steak can be prepared a day ahead. Toast can be made 3 days ahead.
■ Storage: Steak, covered, in refrigerator. Toast rounds, in airtight container.
■ Freeze: Toast rounds suitable.
■ Microwave: Pasta suitable.

SHRIMP TORTELLINI WITH CURRY CREAM

7oz uncooked medium shrimp,
    shelled, deveined
1 quantity plain pasta dough

CURRY CREAM
2 tablespoons (¼ stick) butter
1 tablespoon curry powder
2 green onions, chopped
½ teaspoon ground cumin
1 small fresh red chili pepper,
    chopped
1¼ cups canned unsweetened
    coconut milk
¼ cup water

Chop shrimp finely. Roll pasta dough until ⅛ inch thick, cut 2 inch rounds from dough. Cut rounds in half, top each half with a piece of shrimp, brush edges lightly with water. Fold rounds in half, press edges together to seal.

Just before serving, add tortellini to large pan of boiling water, boil, uncovered, about 3 minutes or until tortellini are tender; drain. Combine tortellini and hot curry cream in bowl.

Curry Cream: Heat butter in pan, add curry powder, onions, cumin and chili, cook, stirring, for 1 minute. Stir in coconut milk and water, bring to boil, simmer, uncovered, for about 5 minutes or until sauce thickens slightly.

Serves 4.

- ■ Tortellini and curry cream can be made a day ahead.
- ■ Storage: Covered, in refrigerator.
- ■ Freeze: Uncooked tortellini suitable.
- ■ Microwave: Not suitable.

CHILI BEEF STIR-FRY IN NOODLE NESTS

¾lb rump steak, thinly sliced
1 teaspoon grated fresh gingerroot
3 tablespoons dry white wine
1 tablespoon olive oil
1 onion, chopped
1 red bell pepper, chopped
1 carrot, sliced
1 teaspoon cornstarch
⅓ cup water
1 small chicken bouillon cube, crumbled
1 tablespoon sambal oelek _Chilli Salt Paste_
1 teaspoon Oriental sesame oil
1 teaspoon dark brown sugar
2 tablespoons tomato ketchup
3 large Swiss chard leaves, shredded

NOODLE NESTS
¼lb capellini egg noodles
2 egg yolks, lightly beaten

Combine steak, gingerroot and wine in bowl; cover, refrigerate 2 hours.

Heat oil in wok or pan, add steak mixture in batches, stir-fry until well browned; remove from wok.

Add onion, pepper and carrot to wok, stir-fry for 2 minutes. Return steak to wok, stir in blended cornstarch and water, bouillon cube, sambal oelek, sesame oil, sugar and ketchup. Stir until mixture boils and thickens slightly, remove from heat; stir in Swiss chard.

Just before serving, spoon hot mixture into hot noodle nests.

Noodle Nests: Add noodles to large pan of boiling water, boil, uncovered, until just tender; drain well.

Combine hot noodles with egg yolks in bowl; mix well. Divide mixture between 6 x 4 inch diameter greased pie tins, bringing noodles up the sides of tins. Place tins on baking sheet, bake in 400°F oven for 30 minutes, gently remove nests from tins, place nests upside down on baking sheet. Bake further 15 minutes or until bases are well browned and crisp.

Makes 6.

- ■ Nests and filling can be prepared 6 hours ahead.
- ■ Storage: Covered, in refrigerator.
- ■ Freeze: Not suitable.
- ■ Microwave: Not suitable.

CHEESE RAVIOLI WITH PECAN AND CILANTRO PESTO

1 quantity plain pasta dough

FILLING
7oz feta cheese, mashed
3½oz ricotta cheese
½ teaspoon ground cinnamon

PECAN AND CILANTRO PESTO
⅓ cup chopped pecan nuts, toasted
2 tablespoons pine nuts, toasted
2 cloves garlic, chopped
½ cup chopped fresh cilantro
¼ cup light sour cream
½ cup olive oil

Cut pasta dough into 4 portions, roll each portion until ⅛ inch thick. Place ½ level teaspoons of filling 1½ inches apart over 2 pasta sheets. Lightly brush remaining sheets of pasta with water, place over filling, press firmly between filling. Cut into 1½ inch square ravioli shapes.

Just before serving, add ravioli to large pan of boiling water, boil, uncovered, about 5 minutes or until tender; drain. Lightly toss hot ravioli with pecan and cilantro pesto.

Filling: Combine cheeses and cinnamon in bowl; beat until smooth.

Pecan and Cilantro Pesto: Blend or process all ingredients until combined.

Serves 6.

- ■ Ravioli and pesto can be made a day ahead.
- ■ Storage: Covered, in refrigerator.
- ■ Freeze: Uncooked ravioli suitable.
- ■ Microwave: Not suitable.

LEFT: From left: Steak Strips with Tomato Tagliatelle, Shrimp Tortellini with Curry Cream.
BELOW: From left: Cheese Ravioli with Pecan and Cilantro Pesto, Chili Beef Stir-Fry in Noodle Nests.

WARM SALMON AND ASPARAGUS SALAD

¾lb piece salmon
1 bunch (½lb) asparagus, chopped
2 tablespoons (¼ stick) butter
1 clove garlic, minced
½lb fettuccine pasta
1 tablespoon butter, melted, extra
3 tablespoons chopped fresh oregano

BASIL SAUCE
½ cup water
2 teaspoons French mustard
3 tablespoons dry white wine
1 tablespoon lemon juice
2½ teaspoons cornstarch
1 tablespoon water, extra
½ cup heavy cream
3 tablespoons shredded fresh basil

Remove skin and bones from salmon, slice salmon thinly. Boil, steam or micro- wave asparagus until just tender; drain. Heat butter in pan, add garlic, cook, stir- ring, 1 minute. Add salmon, cook, stirring gently, about 2 minutes or until just cooked through, stir in asparagus.

Just before serving, add pasta to large pan of boiling water, boil, uncovered, until just tender; drain. Toss pasta with extra butter and oregano. Serve with warm asparagus, salmon mixture and sauce.

Basil Sauce: Combine water, mustard, wine and juice in pan, bring to boil. Stir in blended cornstarch and extra water, stir until sauce boils and thickens slightly. Remove from heat, stir in cream and basil.

Serves 4.

■ Salmon mixture can be prepared 3 hours ahead.
■ Storage: Covered, in refrigerator.
■ Freeze: Not suitable.
■ Microwave: Suitable.

BEEF AND PASTA SALAD WITH CREAMY HORSERADISH

1lb piece beef tenderloin
1 tablespoon olive oil
3 cups (7oz) bow-tie pasta
7oz snow peas
1 red bell pepper, sliced
½lb mini yellow pear tomatoes

CREAMY HORSERADISH
⅓ cup French salad dressing
1 teaspoon horseradish cream
2 tablespoons mayonnaise
1 tablespoon light sour cream
3 tablespoons chopped fresh chives

Trim excess fat from beef. Heat oil in pan, add beef, cook over high heat until well browned all over.

Place beef in roasting pan, bake in 350°F oven about 25 minutes or until medium rare; cool.

Add pasta to large pan of boiling water, boil, uncovered, until just tender, drain, rinse under cold water; drain well.

Boil, steam or microwave peas until just tender; drain. Cut beef into cubes, combine beef cubes with pasta, peas, pepper, tomatoes and creamy horseradish in bowl; toss gently.

Creamy Horseradish: Combine all ingredients in jar; shake well.

Serves 6.

- Salad can be made 3 hours ahead.
- Storage: Covered, in refrigerator.
- Freeze: Not suitable.
- Microwave: Pasta and peas suitable.

GOLDEN PASTA BITES WITH GARLIC MAYONNAISE

2 cups (5½oz) pasta twists
all-purpose flour
2 eggs, lightly beaten
packaged unseasoned bread crumbs
oil for deep-frying

GARLIC MAYONNAISE
3 egg yolks
2 teaspoons dry mustard
1 tablespoon white vinegar
2 cloves garlic, minced
1½ cups olive oil
2 tablespoons finely chopped
**   red bell pepper**
2 tablespoons chopped fresh chives
1 tablespoon chopped fresh parsley

Add pasta to large pan of boiling water, boil, uncovered, until just tender, drain, rinse well under cold water; pat dry with absorbent paper. Lightly toss pasta in flour, shake away excess flour. Dip pasta in eggs then bread crumbs.

Just before serving, deep-fry pasta in hot oil until lightly browned; drain on absorbent paper. Serve hot pasta with garlic mayonnaise.

Garlic Mayonnaise: Blend or process egg yolks, mustard, vinegar and garlic until smooth. With motor operating, add oil gradually in thin stream, blend until thick. Transfer mixture to bowl, stir in pepper and herbs.

Serves 4.

- Pasta can be prepared a day ahead. Mayonnaise can be made a day ahead.
- Storage: Covered, in refrigerator.
- Freeze: Not suitable.
- Microwave: Pasta suitable.

ABOVE LEFT: Clockwise from front: Sherried Ham Pots with Raisin Citrus Sauce, Warm Salmon and Asparagus Salad, Beef and Pasta Salad with Creamy Horseradish.

SHERRIED HAM POTS WITH RAISIN CITRUS SAUCE

¼ quantity plain pasta dough
¾ cup (1½ sticks) butter
10oz leg ham, chopped
1 onion, chopped
4 green onions, chopped
2 teaspoons canned drained
**   green peppercorns**
pinch cayenne pepper
¼ cup sweet sherry
½ cup heavy cream
2½ teaspoons unflavored gelatin
1 tablespoon water

RAISIN CITRUS SAUCE
1 cup water
2½ teaspoons cornstarch
¼ cup port wine jelly
1 teaspoon grated orange zest
¼ cup fresh orange juice
2 tablespoons golden raisins

Lightly oil 6 molds (½ cup capacity). Roll pasta dough until ⅛ inch thick. Add pasta sheet to large pan of boiling water, boil, uncovered, until just tender; drain, cool. Cut 6 x 4½ inch rounds from pasta, line prepared molds with pasta rounds.

Heat butter in pan, add ham, onion, green onions, peppercorns and cayenne,

cook, stirring, until onion is soft. Add sherry and cream, bring to boil, simmer, uncovered, about 5 minutes or until slightly thickened; cool.

Sprinkle gelatin over water in cup, stand in small pan of simmering water, stir until dissolved; cool slightly. Combine ham mixture and gelatin, blend or process mixture until smooth, spoon into molds; cover, refrigerate several hours or until firm.

Just before serving, turn out molds, serve with raisin citrus sauce.

Raisin Citrus Sauce: Blend 2 tablespoons of the water with cornstarch in bowl. Combine remaining water with remaining ingredients in pan, bring to boil, stir in cornstarch mixture, stir until sauce boils and thickens; cover, cool. Refrigerate sauce until cold.

Serves 6.

- Ham pots and sauce can be made 2 days ahead.
- Storage: Covered, in refrigerator.
- Freeze: Not suitable.
- Microwave: Pasta, gelatin and sauce suitable.

BELOW: Golden Pasta Bites with Garlic Mayonnaise.

FRIED PASTA BOW-TIES WITH PORK AND PLUM SAUCE

1 cup (2½oz) bow-tie pasta
all-purpose flour
2 eggs, lightly beaten
packaged unseasoned bread crumbs
oil for deep-frying

PORK AND PLUM SAUCE
2 teaspoons light soy sauce
2 teaspoons hoisin sauce
⅓ cup plum sauce
¼ teaspoon Oriental sesame oil
2 tablespoons plum jam
¼ cup water
¼ teaspoon sambal oelek
1 teaspoon cornstarch
2 teaspoons dry sherry
½lb piece barbequed
    red pork, sliced

Add pasta to large pan of boiling water, boil, uncovered, until just tender, drain well, pat dry with absorbent paper. Toss pasta in flour, shake away excess flour, dip in eggs then bread crumbs. Place crumbed pasta in single layer on tray; cover, refrigerate 1 hour.
Just before serving, deep-fry pasta in hot oil until well browned; drain on absorbent paper, serve with sauce.
Pork and Plum Sauce: Combine sauces, oil, jam, water and sambal oelek in pan. Stir in blended cornstarch and sherry, stir over heat until sauce boils and thickens, stir in pork, cook until pork is heated through.

Serves 4.

■ Pasta can be crumbed a day ahead. Sauce can be made a day ahead.
■ Storage: Covered, in refrigerator.
■ Freeze: Not suitable.
■ Microwave: Pasta and sauce suitable.

SHRIMP AND NOODLE SOUP

2 tablespoons (¼ stick) butter
1 red bell pepper, chopped
1 onion, chopped
1 leek, chopped
2 x 14½oz cans tomatoes
1½ teaspoons grated fresh
    gingerroot
2 small chicken bouillon cubes,
    crumbled
8 cups water
2 tablespoons chopped fresh parsley
tiny pinch saffron
3 tablespoons tomato paste
1 carrot
1 stalk celery
2oz fresh egg noodles
1 teaspoon cracked black
    peppercorns
2 tablespoons lemon juice
2½oz oyster mushrooms
10oz cooked shrimp, shelled

Heat butter in large pan, add pepper, onion and leek, cook, stirring, about 10 minutes or until leek is soft. Stir in undrained crushed tomatoes, gingerroot, bouillon cubes, water, parsley, saffron and paste. Bring to boil, simmer, uncovered, for about 40 minutes or until liquid is reduced by two-thirds. Strain mixture, reserve broth; discard pulp. Cut carrot and celery into strips.
Just before serving, return broth to pan, bring to boil, add carrot, celery, noodles, peppercorns and juice. Simmer, covered, 5 minutes, add mushrooms and shrimp, cook further 2 minutes.

 Serves 4.

■ Recipe can be prepared a day ahead.
■ Storage: Covered, in refrigerator.
■ Freeze: Not suitable.
■ Microwave: Suitable.

LEFT: From left: Fried Pasta Bow-Ties with Pork and Plum Sauce, Shrimp and Noodle Soup.

LEAFY PASTA SQUARES IN BUTTER WITH PARMESAN

½ cup all-purpose flour
3 tablespoons fine semolina
¼ cup finely grated fresh
   Parmesan cheese
1 egg
20 flat-leafed parsley leaves
3½oz fresh Parmesan cheese, extra
3oz (¾ stick) butter

Sift flour and semolina into bowl, stir in grated cheese. Add egg, stir until combined (or process all ingredients until smooth). Turn dough onto lightly floured surface, knead until smooth. Roll dough through pasta machine, following manufacturer's instructions, until ⅛ inch thick. Lay pasta sheet on bench, press leaves over half the pasta, fold pasta in half crossways over leaves. Roll pasta through machine once, cut pasta into 1¼ inch squares.

Just before serving, add pasta to large pan of boiling water, boil, uncovered, until just tender; drain.

Use vegetable peeler to shave strips from extra Parmesan. Melt butter in pan, add pasta, heat through. Serve pasta topped with strips of Parmesan.

Serves 4.

■ Squares can be made 6 hours ahead.
■ Storage: Covered, in refrigerator.
■ Freeze: Uncooked pasta suitable.
■ Microwave: Pasta suitable.

CHICKEN AND FENNEL SHELLS WITH CHILI CHIVE DRESSING

3 large carrots
1 cup water
1 small chicken bouillon cube,
   crumbled
2 boneless, skinless chicken
   breast halves
12 extra large pasta shells

FENNEL FILLING
2 tablespoons (¼ stick) butter
2 onions, finely chopped
1 cup finely chopped fennel bulb
⅔ cup creamed ricotta cheese
3 tablespoons chopped fresh
   fennel leaves
3 tablespoons chopped pitted
   black olives

CHILI CHIVE DRESSING
½ cup olive oil
2 tablespoons red wine vinegar
1 teaspoon sweet chili sauce
1 teaspoon sugar
1 tablespoon orange juice
1 tablespoon chopped fresh chives

Using vegetable peeler, cut carrots into thin ribbons. Add carrots to pan of boiling water, drain immediately, rinse under cold water; drain.

Combine water and bouillon cube in pan, bring to boil. Add chicken, simmer, covered, about 5 minutes or until chicken is just tender, drain; cool. Cut chicken into thin strips, combine with carrots.

Just before serving, add pasta to large pan of boiling water, boil, uncovered, until just tender; drain. Spoon filling into each shell, serve shells over carrot and chicken; top with dressing.

Fennel Filling: Heat butter in pan, add onions and fennel bulb, cook over low heat, stirring occasionally, about 10 minutes or until onions are lightly browned and soft. Combine onion mixture with cheese, fennel leaves and olives.

Chili Chive Dressing: Combine all ingredients in jar; shake well.

Serves 4.

■ Can be prepared a day ahead.
■ Storage: Covered, in refrigerator.
■ Freeze: Not suitable.
■ Microwave: Suitable.

LEFT: From left: Leafy Pasta Squares in Butter with Parmesan, Chicken and Fennel Shells with Chili Chive Dressing.
ABOVE RIGHT: Roast Duck with Tangy Marmalade Sauce.

ROAST DUCK WITH TANGY MARMALADE SAUCE

½ cup fresh orange juice
2 teaspoons hoisin sauce
¼ teaspoon five-spice powder
2 large (1lb) boneless duck
    breast halves
6 Chinese dried mushrooms
1 cup boiling water
2 small chicken bouillon
    cubes, crumbled
1 tablespoon orange marmalade
1 teaspoon cornstarch
2 teaspoons Grand Marnier
3½oz snow peas
½lb lasagnette pasta

Combine juice, sauce and spice powder in bowl, add duck; cover, refrigerate several hours or overnight, turning duck over occasionally.

Just before serving, remove duck from marinade; reserve marinade. Place duck on wire rack over roasting pan , bake in 400°F oven about 15 minutes or until duck is well browned and tender; remove from oven, slice thinly.

While duck is cooking, place mushrooms in bowl, cover with the boiling water, stand 20 minutes. Drain mushrooms, reserve liquid; discard stems, slice caps thinly. Combine mushrooms, reserved liquid, reserved marinade, bouillon cubes and marmalade in pan. Bring to

boil, simmer, covered, for 5 minutes. Stir in blended cornstarch and liqueur, stir until sauce boils and thickens.

Boil, steam or microwave peas until just tender; drain. Add pasta to large pan of boiling water, boil, uncovered, until just tender; drain. Combine pasta and peas, serve with duck and mushrooms, drizzle with hot sauce.

Serves 6.

■ Can be prepared 2 days ahead.
■ Storage: Covered, in refrigerator.
■ Freeze: Not suitable.
■ Microwave: Pasta and snow
    peas suitable.

CRISP PEPPER PASTA WITH PEPPER BEEF FILLING

⅓ cup finely grated gruyere cheese
¼ cup finely grated cheddar cheese
¼ teaspoon canned drained green
   peppercorns, crushed
1 teaspoon water, approximately
1 teaspoon olive oil
1 small onion, chopped
3½oz ground beef
1½ teaspoons tomato paste
1 tablespoon water, extra
1 small beef bouillon cube, crumbled
½ teaspoon sugar
1 egg, separated
⅓ quantity pepper pasta dough
all-purpose flour
oil for shallow-frying

PORT WINE SAUCE
½ cup port wine
1 teaspoon canned drained
   green peppercorns
1 cup heavy cream
2 teaspoons cornstarch
2 teaspoons water

Combine cheeses and peppercorns in bowl with enough water to make ingredients cling together. Heat olive oil in pan, add onion, cook, stirring, until soft. Add beef, cook, stirring, until well browned. Stir in combined paste, extra water, bouillon cube and sugar, cook for 3 minutes; cool. Stir in egg white.

Roll pasta dough until ⅛ inch thick, cut into 3 inch rounds. Add rounds to large pan of boiling water, boil, uncovered, until just tender; drain well.

Toss rounds in flour, shake away excess flour. Top each round with ½ level teaspoon of cheese mixture and 1 level teaspoon of meat mixture. Brush edges of rounds with egg yolk, fold in half, press edges together firmly.

Just before serving, shallow-fry in hot oil until lightly browned; drain on absorbent paper. Serve with hot sauce.

Port Wine Sauce: Bring port wine to boil in pan, simmer, uncovered, until reduced by one-third. Stir in peppercorns, cream and blended cornstarch and water, stir until sauce boils and thickens.

Serves 6.

■ Can be prepared 2 days ahead.
■ Storage: Covered, in refrigerator.
■ Freeze: Sauce suitable.
■ Microwave: Sauce suitable.

TASTY LITTLE HAM, CHEESE AND PASTA CUPS

2 cups water
2 small chicken bouillon
   cubes, crumbled
¼lb linguine pasta
1 cup (3½oz) finely grated
   pecorino cheese
3½oz cooked leg ham, finely chopped
½ cup coarsely grated carrot
2 tablespoons chopped fresh parsley
1 tablespoon chopped fresh chives
3 tablespoons chopped stuffed olives
4 eggs, lightly beaten
1½ cups milk

Lightly grease 6 molds (¾ cup capacity). Combine water and bouillon cubes in pan, bring to boil, add pasta, boil, uncovered, until just tender; cool pasta in broth.

Combine cheese, ham, carrot, herbs, olives, eggs and milk in large bowl. Add undrained pasta mixture, stir until just combined. Divide mixture between prepared molds. Stand molds in roasting pan, pour in enough boiling water to come halfway up sides of molds. Bake, uncovered, in 350°F oven about 1 hour or until firm; cool to room temperature before turning onto plates.

Serves 6.

■ Cups can be made 6 hours ahead.
■ Storage: Covered, at room
   temperature.
■ Freeze: Not suitable.
■ Microwave: Not suitable.

SMOKED CHICKEN AND PASTA TERRINE

1 leek
3 x 3in x 7in dried lasagne pasta sheets
¼ cup olive oil
1 clove garlic, minced
¼ cup tomato paste
1 teaspoon sugar
3oz button mushrooms, sliced
2 large tomatoes, peeled, seeded
½ cup pitted black olives, sliced
1 tablespoon drained chopped capers
½ teaspoon dried marjoram leaves
¼ cup all-purpose flour
¼ cup water
1½ cups (5oz) shredded mozzarella cheese
¾lb boneless, skinless smoked chicken breasts, sliced

BASIL DRESSING
1½ cups olive oil
⅓ cup lemon juice
2 tablespoons shredded fresh basil
1 small red bell pepper, chopped

Lightly grease 4½ inch x 10 inch oven-proof glass loaf dish. Wash leek, drop 6 outer leaves of leek into pan of boiling water, boil 3 minutes, drain. Thinly slice white section of remaining leek.

Add pasta to large pan of boiling water, boil, uncovered, until just tender, drain, rinse under cold water; drain well.

Heat oil in pan, add sliced leek and garlic, cook, stirring, until leek is soft. Add paste, sugar, mushrooms, tomatoes, olives, capers and marjoram. Cook, covered, for 5 minutes, stirring occasionally. Stir in blended flour and water, stir until mixture boils and thickens; cover, cool.

Line base and sides of prepared dish with boiled leek leaves, allowing ends to overhang sides of dish.

Combine cheese and chicken, divide mixture into 4 portions. Sprinkle 1 portion of cheese mixture over base of dish. Trim pasta to fit dish, place a layer of pasta over cheese mixture. Spread with one-third of tomato mixture, top with another portion of cheese mixture. Repeat layering, ending with cheese mixture. Fold leek leaves over to cover cheese mixture, cover dish with greased foil. Bake in 350°F oven about 1½ hours or until firm to touch; cool, refrigerate overnight.

Just before serving, turn terrine out, serve sliced with dressing.

Basil Dressing: Combine all ingredients in jar; shake well.

Serves 6.

■ Terrine can be made 2 days ahead. Dressing can be made a day ahead.
■ Storage: Covered, in refrigerator.
■ Freeze: Not suitable.
■ Microwave: Leek and pasta suitable.

LEFT: From left: Crisp Pepper Pasta with Pepper Beef Filling, Tasty Little Ham, Cheese and Pasta Cups.
BELOW: Smoked Chicken and Pasta Terrine.

POULTRY & RABBIT

In this section, we have used chicken, Rock Cornish hens, quail, duck and rabbit in innovative main meals for the family and for entertaining. There are taste treats of many kinds: plump little ravioli and tortellini with delicious fillings, simple baked or fried dishes, curries, stir-fries, casseroles, salads and more. Most are saucy, and all include pasta as part of the dish or as an accompaniment.

CHICKEN SAVARIN WITH CREAMY CURRY SAUCE

7oz spinach lasagne pasta sheets
6 boneless, skinless chicken breast halves, chopped
2 egg whites
2 teaspoons brandy
1¼ cups heavy cream
1 tablespoon chopped fresh chives
2 teaspoons canned drained green peppercorns, crushed

CREAMY CURRY SAUCE
2 tablespoons (¼ stick) butter
2 teaspoons curry powder
2 teaspoons all-purpose flour
¾ cup milk
½ small chicken bouillon cube, crumbled
2oz packaged cream cheese

Line 9 inch savarin pan with plastic wrap. Add pasta to large pan of boiling water, boil, uncovered, until just tender, drain; pat dry with absorbent paper.

Line prepared pan with pasta sheets, overlapping edges, allowing excess pasta to overhang side of pan.

Process chicken, egg whites and brandy until smooth. Add cream, process until just combined; stir in chives and peppercorns. Spread chicken mixture evenly into pan, fold overhanging pasta over mixture, trim edges.

Cover pan with plastic wrap, then foil. Place pan in roasting pan, pour enough boiling water into dish to come halfway up side of pan. Bake in 350°F oven about 1½ hours or until firm to touch.

Stand savarin in pan 5 minutes before turning out. Serve with sauce.

Creamy Curry Sauce: Heat butter in pan, stir in curry powder and flour, stir over heat until bubbling. Remove from heat, gradually stir in milk, bouillon cube and cheese, stir over heat until mixture boils and thickens. Blend or process sauce until smooth.

Serves 6.

- Savarin and sauce can be made a day ahead.
- Storage: Covered, in refrigerator.
- Freeze: Not suitable
- Microwave: Sauce suitable.

RED CHICKEN CURRY WITH RICE VERMICELLI

½lb rice vermicelli
oil for deep-frying
2 tablespoons oil, extra
2½lb chicken thighs, boned, skinned, chopped
½ cup canned unsweetened coconut cream
2 tablespoons chopped fresh cilantro

RED CURRY PASTE
1 small red onion, chopped
2 cloves garlic, minced
1 teaspoon chopped fresh cilantro root
1½ teaspoons dried chili flakes
2 teaspoons grated fresh gingerroot
1 teaspoon grated lime zest
2 tablespoons lime juice
1 tablespoon paprika
1 teaspoon ground cumin

Deep-fry vermicelli in hot oil in batches until puffed; drain on absorbent paper.

Heat extra oil in wok or pan, add curry paste, cook, stirring, for 1 minute. Add chicken in batches, stir-fry until chicken is cooked through. Stir in coconut cream and cilantro, bring to boil, simmer, uncovered, about 5 minutes or until thickened. Serve curry over vermicelli.

Curry Paste: Blend or process all ingredients until smooth.

Serves 6.

- Curry can be made a day ahead. Paste can be made a week ahead.
- Storage: Covered, in refrigerator.
- Freeze: Not suitable.
- Microwave: Not suitable.

RIGHT: From left: Chicken Savarin with Creamy Curry Sauce, Red Chicken Curry with Rice Vermicelli.

ROAST ROCK CORNISH HENS WITH PROSCIUTTO SAUCE

3 x ¾lb Rock Cornish hens
2 tablespoons olive oil
1lb lasagnette pasta

PROSCIUTTO SAUCE
2 tablespoons olive oil
2 tablespoons (¼ stick) butter
2 onions, chopped
2 cloves garlic, minced
2 stalks celery, chopped
1 carrot, chopped
1 red bell pepper, chopped
3½oz prosciutto, chopped
2 x 14½oz cans tomatoes
½ cup dry red wine
2 tablespoons tomato paste
3 tablespoons chopped fresh basil

Cut hens into quarters, place on wire rack over roasting pan, brush hens with oil, bake in 375°F oven about 20 minutes or until cooked through.

Add pasta to large pan of boiling water, boil, uncovered, until just tender; drain. Serve hens with pasta and sauce.

Prosciutto Sauce: Heat oil and butter in pan, add onions, garlic, celery, carrot, pepper and prosciutto, cook, stirring, for about 5 minutes or until vegetables are soft. Stir in undrained crushed tomatoes, wine and paste, bring to boil, simmer, uncovered, for about 10 minutes or until sauce is thickened; stir in basil.

Serves 6.

■ Sauce can be made a day ahead.
■ Storage: Covered, in refrigerator.
■ Freeze: Not suitable.
■ Microwave: Pasta suitable.

LEMONY CHICKEN AND ANCHOVY RAVIOLI

2 teaspoons olive oil
½lb ground chicken
4 anchovy fillets, chopped
3 tablespoons grated fresh Parmesan cheese
1 tablespoon heavy cream
¼ teaspoon ground nutmeg
1 teaspoon grated lemon zest
2 tablespoons lemon juice
¼ cup chopped fresh parsley
1 quantity plain pasta dough
2oz fresh Parmesan cheese, thinly sliced, extra

CREAMY CHEESE SAUCE
2 tablespoons (¼ stick) butter
2 tablespoons all-purpose flour
1 cup water
**1 small chicken bouillon cube,
    crumbled**
1¼ cups heavy cream
**3 tablespoons grated fresh
    Parmesan cheese**

Heat oil in pan, add chicken, cook, stirring, for 2 minutes. Stir in anchovies, cheese, cream, nutmeg, zest, juice and parsley. Blend or process mixture until smooth.

Divide pasta dough in half, roll each piece until ⅛ inch thick. Place ¼ level teaspoons of filling 1¼ inches apart over 1 sheet of pasta. Lightly brush remaining pasta sheet with water, place over filling; press firmly between filling. Cut into square ravioli shapes. Lightly sprinkle ravioli with a little flour.

Just before serving, add ravioli to large pan of boiling water, boil, uncovered, for about 5 minutes or until just tender; drain. Combine ravioli with hot sauce; serve topped with extra cheese.

Creamy Cheese Sauce: Melt butter in pan, add flour, stir over heat until bubbling. Remove from heat, gradually stir in com-bined water and bouillon cube, stir over heat until mixture boils and thickens. Simmer, uncovered, until reduced by half. Just before serving, stir in cream and cheese. Serves 4.

◼ Ravioli and sauce can be made a day ahead.
◼ Storage: Covered, in refrigerator.
◼ Freeze: Uncooked ravioli suitable.
◼ Microwave: Not suitable.

CHICKEN JAMBALAYA

**4 boneless, skinless chicken
    breast halves**
2 tablespoons olive oil
1 onion, chopped
1 clove garlic, minced
1 small green bell pepper, chopped
14½oz can tomatoes
2 small chicken bouillon cubes, crumbled
2 cups water
1 cup orzo pasta
¼ teaspoon chili powder
½ teaspoon seasoned pepper
¼ teaspoon dried thyme leaves
3½oz cooked leg ham, chopped
¼ cup pitted black olives, chopped

Cut chicken into ½ inch strips. Heat oil in pan, add chicken, cook, stirring, until lightly browned and cooked; drain chicken on absorbent paper.

Add onion, garlic and bell pepper to pan, cook, stirring, until onion is soft. Stir in undrained crushed tomatoes, bouillon cubes, water, pasta, chili, seasoned pepper and thyme. Bring to boil, simmer, covered, about 10 minutes or until pasta is tender.

Add chicken, ham and olives to pan, simmer, covered, further 10 minutes or until most of the liquid has been absorbed. Serves 4.

◼ Recipe can be made a day ahead.
◼ Storage: Covered, in refrigerator.
◼ Freeze: Suitable.
◼ Microwave: Suitable.

*LEFT: From back: Roast Rock Cornish Hens with Prosciutto Sauce, Lemony Chicken and Anchovy Ravioli.
BELOW: Chicken Jambalaya.*

CHICKEN TORTELLINI WITH CREAMY TOMATO SAUCE

2 quantities plain pasta dough
1 egg white, lightly beaten

FILLING
1¼lb chicken thighs, boned, skinned
2 egg yolks
3 tablespoons chopped fresh basil
½ teaspoon cracked black peppercorns

CREAMY TOMATO SAUCE
1 tablespoon olive oil
1 small onion, chopped
1 clove garlic, minced
14½oz can tomatoes
3 tablespoons dry red wine
1 tablespoon chopped fresh basil
½ teaspoon sugar
¼ teaspoon ground black peppercorns
1 cup heavy cream

Roll pasta dough until ⅛ inch thick, cut into 2¼ inch squares. Brush edges of squares with egg white, top each square with ½ level teaspoon of filling, fold squares in half diagonally, press edges together firmly. Overlap corners of each tortellini, press firmly.

Just before serving, add tortellini to large pan of boiling water, boil, uncovered, about 4 minutes or until tender. Serve tortellini with sauce.

Filling: Trim excess fat from chicken, process chicken until finely ground. Combine chicken, egg yolks, basil and pepper in bowl; mix well.

Creamy Tomato Sauce: Heat oil in pan, add onion and garlic, cook, stirring, until onion is soft. Stir in undrained crushed tomatoes, wine, basil, sugar and peppercorns, bring to boil. Blend or process mixture until smooth, return to pan. Stir in cream, cook until heated through.

Serves 4.

■ Tortellini and sauce can be prepared a day ahead.
■ Storage: Covered, in refrigerator.
■ Freeze: Uncooked tortellini suitable.
■ Microwave: Not suitable.

CHILI CHICKEN AND PASTA STIR-FRY

1¼lb chicken thighs, boned, skinned
all-purpose flour
oil for deep-frying
1 tablespoon olive oil
1 onion, chopped
1 clove garlic, minced
1 small fresh red chili pepper, finely chopped
2 stalks lemon grass, chopped
1 cup (2½oz) pasta twists
3 tablespoons fish sauce
⅓ cup canned, unsweetened coconut milk
¼ cup shredded fresh basil

Cut chicken into thin strips, toss chicken in flour, shake away excess flour. Deep-fry chicken in hot oil until lightly browned; drain on absorbent paper.

Heat olive oil in wok or pan, add onion, garlic, chili and lemon grass, stir-fry until onion is soft.

Add pasta to large pan of boiling water, boil, uncovered, until just tender; drain.

Add pasta, sauce, coconut milk and basil to pan, stir until heated through.

Serves 4.

■ Best made just before serving.
■ Freeze: Not suitable.
■ Microwave: Pasta suitable.

CRUMBED FRIED CHICKEN WITH SPICY PEANUT SAUCE

7oz fettuccine pasta
1 carrot
½ small leek
1 small red bell pepper
4 boneless, skinless chicken breast halves
all-purpose flour
2 eggs, lightly beaten
packaged unseasoned bread crumbs
¼ cup olive oil

SPICY PEANUT SAUCE
3 tablespoons olive oil
1 onion, finely chopped
1 clove garlic, minced
2 teaspoons curry powder
½ teaspoon turmeric
1 cup water
1 teaspoon white vinegar
2 teaspoons sugar
¼ cup smooth peanut butter

Add pasta to large pan of boiling water, boil, uncovered, until just tender, drain; keep warm. Cut carrot, leek and pepper into thin strips.

Toss chicken in flour, shake away excess flour. Dip chicken in eggs, then bread crumbs.

Just before serving, heat oil in pan, add chicken, cook until well browned and cooked through. Serve hot with pasta, uncooked vegetable strips and hot sauce.

Spicy Peanut Sauce: Heat oil in pan, add onion and garlic, cook, stirring, until onion is soft. Stir in curry and turmeric, cook 1 minute. Stir in water, vinegar, sugar and peanut butter, stir until sauce boils and thickens.

Serves 4.

■ Chicken can be crumbed a day ahead. Sauce can be made a day ahead.
■ Storage: Covered, in refrigerator.
■ Freeze: Not suitable.
■ Microwave: Pasta suitable.

LEFT: Clockwise from left: Chicken Tortellini with Creamy Tomato Sauce, Chili Chicken and Pasta Stir-Fry, Crumbed Fried Chicken with Spicy Peanut Sauce.

BAKED QUAIL WITH NUTTY BACON SEASONING

2 cups dry red wine
1 cup olive oil
2 cloves garlic, minced
2 tablespoons chopped fresh sage
8 quail
2 cups (½lb) mini bow-tie pasta

NUTTY BACON SEASONING
½lb slices bacon, chopped
3 tablespoons chopped fresh chives
½ cup fresh bread crumbs
¼ cup pine nuts, toasted

Combine wine, oil, garlic and sage in bowl, add quail; cover, refrigerate several hours or overnight, turning occasionally.

Remove quail from marinade, reserve 1 cup of marinade. Spoon seasoning into quail cavities, secure legs with kitchen string. Place quail on wire rack in roasting pan, bake in 350°F oven about 35 minutes or until cooked through.

Add pasta to large pan of boiling water, boil, uncovered, until just tender; drain. Bring reserved marinade to boil in pan, combine with pasta. Serve quail with pasta.

Nutty Bacon Seasoning: Combine bacon, chives, bread crumbs and nuts in bowl; mix well.

Serves 4.

■ Can be prepared a day ahead.
■ Storage: Covered, in refrigerator.
■ Freeze: Not suitable.
■ Microwave: Pasta suitable.

CREAMY HERBED CHICKEN WITH SPINACH SPAGHETTI

4 boneless, skinless chicken breast
    halves, sliced
2 teaspoons paprika
1 teaspoon cracked black
    peppercorns
8oz package cream cheese
⅓ cup grated fresh Parmesan cheese
1 cup water
1 small chicken bouillon cube,
    crumbled
2 tablespoons chopped fresh basil
2 tablespoons chopped fresh parsley
1 tablespoon chopped fresh mint
2 tablespoons (¼ stick) butter
1lb spinach spaghetti pasta

Combine chicken, paprika and peppercorns in bowl; stand 20 minutes.

Blend or process cheeses, water, bouillon cube and herbs until almost smooth. Melt butter in pan, add chicken mixture, cook, stirring, over high heat until well browned. Add cheese mixture, bring to boil, simmer, uncovered, for 5 minutes.

Add pasta to large pan of boiling water, boil, uncovered, until just tender; drain. Serve pasta with creamy chicken.

Serves 6.

■ Best made just before serving.
■ Freeze: Not suitable.
■ Microwave: Pasta suitable.

CREAMY ONION CHICKEN ON LINGUINE

1 tablespoon olive oil
1 tablespoon butter
1 clove garlic, minced
6 boneless, skinless chicken
    breast halves
1lb linguine pasta
1 onion, chopped
1 small chicken bouillon cube,
    crumbled
½ cup water
1¼ cups heavy cream
6 green onions, chopped
1 cup (3½oz) grated pecorino cheese

Heat oil, butter and garlic in pan, add chicken, cook on both sides until tender. Remove from pan, slice thinly; keep warm. Reserve oil mixture in pan.

Add pasta to large pan of boiling water, boil, uncovered, until just tender; drain.

Reheat oil mixture in pan, add onion, cook, stirring, until onion is soft. Add bouillon cube and water, bring to boil, simmer, uncovered, until reduced by half. Add cream, green onions and cheese, stir until cheese has melted. Serve chicken on pasta, top with sauce.

Serves 6.

■ Recipe best made close to serving.
■ Freeze: Not suitable.
■ Microwave: Pasta suitable.

LEFT: From back: Baked Quail with Nutty Bacon Seasoning, Creamy Herbed Chicken with Spinach Spaghetti.
ABOVE: Creamy Onion Chicken on Linguine.

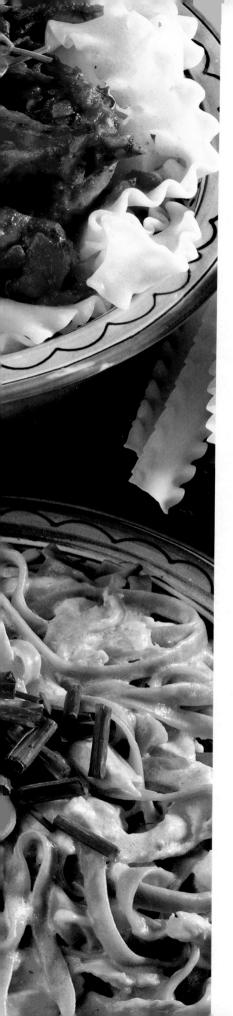

RABBIT IN RED WINE AND GARLIC SAUCE

2lb rabbit
1 cup dry red wine
1 tablespoon dark brown sugar
3 bay leaves
4 cloves garlic, sliced
2 tablespoons chopped fresh thyme
3 tablespoons olive oil
1 onion, chopped
7oz prosciutto, chopped
14½oz can tomatoes
3 tablespoons tomato paste
1lb lasagnette pasta

Cut rabbit into 8 portions, combine with wine, sugar, bay leaves, garlic and thyme in bowl. Cover, refrigerate 2 hours, stirring occasionally.

Remove rabbit from marinade, drain well; reserve marinade. Heat oil in pan, add rabbit, cook until well browned all over, remove from pan. Add onion and prosciutto to pan, cook, stirring, until onion is soft. Add undrained crushed tomatoes and paste, cook, stirring, for 3 minutes. Stir in reserved marinade, bring to boil, boil 2 minutes. Return rabbit to pan, simmer, covered, for 1 hour, remove cover, simmer further 15 minutes or until sauce is thickened.

Add pasta to large pan of boiling water, boil, uncovered, until just tender; drain. Serve pasta with rabbit and sauce.

Serves 4.

- Rabbit can be cooked 2 days ahead.
- Storage: Covered, in refrigerator.
- Freeze: Not suitable.
- Microwave: Pasta suitable.

ROCK CORNISH HENS IN SAFFRON CREAM

2 x 1lb Rock Cornish hens
1 tablespoon olive oil
1lb spinach tagliatelle pasta
¼ cup chopped fresh chives

SAFFRON CREAM
3oz (¾ stick) butter
⅔ cup grated fresh Parmesan cheese
1¼ cups heavy cream
tiny pinch saffron powder

Cut hens in half through backbones and breastbones, place on wire rack over roasting pan, brush with oil. Bake in 350°F oven about 30 minutes or until cooked through; cool.

Remove meat from hens, slice finely. Add pasta to large pan of boiling water, boil, uncovered, until just tender; drain. Return pasta to pan; keep warm.

Combine saffron cream, pasta and hens, serve sprinkled with chives.
Saffron Cream: Melt butter in separate pan, add cheese, cream and saffron, bring to boil, simmer, uncovered, about 5 minutes or until mixture thickens slightly.

Serves 6.

- Hens can be cooked a day ahead. Saffron cream best made just before serving.
- Storage: Covered, in refrigerator.
- Freeze: Not suitable.
- Microwave: Pasta suitable.

CHICKEN SALAD WITH FRESH THYME DRESSING

2 boneless, skinless chicken breast halves
1 cup (¼lb) fresh or frozen green peas
1 quantity plain pasta dough

FRESH THYME DRESSING
2 egg yolks
2 tablespoons cider vinegar
1 cup olive oil
1 tablespoon chopped fresh thyme

Poach, steam or microwave chicken until tender, cool; cut into thin strips. Boil, steam or microwave peas until tender, drain; cool.

Roll pasta dough until ⅛ inch thick, cut into 1¼ inch ribbons. Add pasta to large pan of boiling water, boil, uncovered, about 3 minutes or until just tender; drain. Rinse pasta under cold water; drain. Combine chicken, pasta, peas and dressing in bowl; mix gently.
Fresh Thyme Dressing: Blend or process egg yolks and vinegar until smooth. Add oil gradually in thin stream while motor is operating, blend until thick. Stir in thyme.

Serves 4.

- Can be prepared 2 hours ahead.
- Storage: Covered, in refrigerator.
- Freeze: Not suitable.
- Microwave: Suitable.

LEFT: Clockwise from left: Chicken Salad with Fresh Thyme Dressing, Rabbit in Red Wine and Garlic Sauce, Rock Cornish Hens in Saffron Cream.

WHOLE-WHEAT PASTA STRIPS WITH RABBIT SAUCE

6oz slices bacon
1 onion, chopped
2 cloves garlic, minced
2lb rabbit
8 baby carrots
2 stalks celery, sliced
2 cups water
1 large chicken bouillon
    cube, crumbled
⅔ cup dry white wine
1 quantity whole-wheat pasta dough
2 teaspoons cornstarch
1 tablespoon water, extra
3 tablespoons chopped
    fresh parsley

Cut bacon into ¾ inch strips, add to pan, cook, stirring, until well browned. Add onion and garlic, cook, stirring, until onion

is soft. Cut rabbit into 8 portions, add to pan, cook, stirring, until rabbit is browned all over. Stir in carrots, celery, water, bouillon cube and wine, bring to boil, simmer, covered, about 1½ hours or until tender.

Roll pasta dough until ⅛ inch thick, cut into 1¼ inch x 12 inch strips. Add strips to large pan of boiling water, boil, uncovered, about 5 minutes or until just tender; drain.

Remove rabbit meat from bones, return meat to pan. Stir in blended cornstarch and extra water, stir until mixture boils and thickens slightly. Serve sauce over pasta, sprinkle with parsley.

Serves 4.

■ Sauce can be made 2 days ahead.
■ Storage: Covered, in refrigerator.
■ Freeze: Sauce suitable.
■ Microwave: Pasta suitable.

SHERRIED RABBIT HOTPOT WITH SPINACH FETTUCCINE

2½lb rabbit cutlets
¼ cup olive oil
2 cloves garlic, minced
6oz slices bacon, chopped
2 x 14½oz cans tomatoes
¼ cup tomato paste
2 teaspoons sugar
1 small fresh red chili pepper,
    chopped
2 bay leaves
½ teaspoon dried oregano leaves
¼ cup sweet sherry
10oz broccoli, chopped
¼lb button mushrooms
½lb spinach fettuccine pasta

Remove rabbit meat from bones, chop meat into small pieces. Heat oil in pan, add meat, garlic and bacon, cook, stirring,

ROAST DUCK WITH TOMATO NOODLE NESTS

2 x 2¾lb ducks
2 tablespoons (¼ stick) butter, melted

NOODLE NESTS
½lb fresh egg noodles
oil for deep-frying

TOMATO WINE SAUCE
2 tablespoons (¼ stick) butter
1 onion, sliced
2 tomatoes, peeled, seeded
½ cup dry red wine
½ cup water
¼ cup tomato paste
2 teaspoons Worcestershire sauce

Place ducks in roasting pan, brush with butter. Prick skin all over without piercing meat. Bake in 350°F oven about 1½ hours, basting occasionally with pan juices, until ducks are cooked through.

Cut ducks into quarters, serve hot with noodle nests filled with hot sauce.

Noodle Nests: Arrange quarter of the noodles in thin layer over inside of lightly oiled double strainer. Press top strainer onto noodles. Lower strainer into hot oil, holding handles firmly together, deep-fry until noodles are well browned; drain.

Carefully remove basket from strainer. Repeat with remaining noodles.

Tomato Wine Sauce: Melt butter in pan, add onion, cook, stirring, until soft. Add roughly chopped tomatoes, wine, water, paste and sauce. Bring to boil, simmer, uncovered, about 20 minutes or until slightly thickened.

Serves 4.

- ■ Noodle nests and sauce can be made a day ahead.
- ■ Storage: Separately, covered, in refrigerator.
- ■ Freeze: Sauce suitable.
- ■ Microwave: Sauce suitable.

for 5 minutes. Add undrained crushed tomatoes, paste, sugar, chili, bay leaves, oregano and sherry. Bring to boil, simmer, covered, about 1¼ hours or until rabbit is tender. Add broccoli and mushrooms, cook 5 minutes or until broccoli is just tender. Discard bay leaves.

Add pasta to large pan of boiling water, boil, uncovered, until just tender; drain. Serve rabbit mixture with pasta.

Serves 4.

- ■ Hotpot can be made 2 days ahead.
- ■ Storage: Covered, in refrigerator.
- ■ Freeze: Not suitable.
- ■ Microwave: Pasta suitable.

ABOVE: From left: Whole-Wheat Pasta Strips with Rabbit Sauce, Sherried Rabbit Hotpot with Spinach Fettuccine.
RIGHT: Roast Duck with Tomato Noodle Nests.

HERBED CHICKEN AND PASTA SALAD

1¼ cups (¼lb) vegetable pasta twists
2 cups water
2 small chicken bouillon cubes, crumbled
4 boneless, skinless chicken breast halves
½ cup canned drained pimientos, sliced
½ cup pitted black olives

DRESSING
1 clove garlic, minced
¼ cup red wine vinegar
½ cup olive oil
¼ teaspoon cracked black peppercorns
3 tablespoons shredded fresh basil

Add pasta to large pan of boiling water, boil; uncovered, until just tender; drain. Rinse pasta under cold water; drain.

Combine water and bouillon cubes in pan, bring to boil, add chicken, simmer, covered, about 10 minutes or until cooked through; drain, cool. Cut chicken into ½ inch strips.

Combine chicken, pasta, pimientos and olives in bowl, add dressing, toss to combine. Cover salad, refrigerate several hours before serving.

Dressing: Combine all ingredients in jar; shake well.

Serves 4.

■ Salad can be made a day ahead.
■ Storage: Covered, in refrigerator.
■ Freeze: Not suitable.
■ Microwave: Pasta suitable.

CREAMY CHICKEN, PASTA AND ASPARAGUS CASSEROLE

½lb fettuccine pasta
2 tablespoons olive oil
1 onion, chopped
1 cup (5oz) chopped cooked chicken
1 red bell pepper, chopped
2 stalks celery, chopped
1 small chicken bouillon cube, crumbled
1 cup water
1¼ cups sour cream
15oz can asparagus cuts, drained
½ teaspoon dried oregano leaves
1 cup (¼lb) grated cheddar cheese

Add pasta to large pan of boiling water, boil, uncovered, until just tender; drain. Rinse pasta under cold water; drain well.

Heat oil in large pan, add onion, cook, stirring, until soft. Add chicken, pepper, celery, bouillon cube and water, bring to boil, simmer 5 minutes. Add cream, asparagus and oregano, cook until heated through.

Spoon half the chicken mixture over base of greased ovenproof dish (7 cup capacity), top with pasta, then remaining chicken mixture. Sprinkle with cheese, bake in a 350°F oven about 30 minutes or until cheese is lightly browned.

Serves 4.

■ Recipe can be made a day ahead.
■ Storage: Covered, in refrigerator.
■ Freeze: Not suitable.
■ Microwave: Pasta suitable.

LEFT: From left: Creamy Chicken, Pasta and Asparagus Casserole, Herbed Chicken and Pasta Salad.

DUCK AND PASTA SOUFFLES

¾lb tagliatelle pasta
2 boneless, skinless duck breast
  halves, thinly sliced
3 tablespoons plum sauce
1 tablespoon hoisin sauce
3 tablespoons olive oil
2 small carrots, coarsely grated
¼lb button mushrooms, sliced
2 bunches (1lb) fresh
  asparagus, sliced
1 teaspoon Oriental sesame oil
1 tablespoon light soy sauce
3 eggs, separated
¼ teaspoon five-spice powder

Grease 8 ovenproof dishes (1¼ cup capacity). Add pasta to large pan of boiling water, boil, uncovered, until just tender; drain. Combine duck, plum and hoisin sauces in bowl; cover, refrigerate 2 hours.

Heat half the oil in pan, add duck mixture, cook, stirring, until lightly browned. Remove from pan, drain on absorbent paper. Add remaining oil to pan, add carrots, mushrooms and asparagus, cook, stirring, for 2 minutes. Stir in half the pasta, duck mixture, sesame oil and soy sauce, stir until heated through. Divide mixture between prepared dishes.

Combine remaining pasta with egg yolks and spice in bowl. Beat egg whites in small bowl until soft peaks form, fold into pasta mixture. Spoon into dishes, place on baking sheet, bake in 350°F oven about 15 minutes or until puffed.

Serves 8.

■ Best made just before serving.
■ Freeze: Not suitable.
■ Microwave: Pasta suitable.

ONION AND RABBIT RAVIOLI WITH FRESH PARMESAN

3oz (¾ stick) butter
3 large (1lb) onions, thinly sliced
1 large carrot, grated
2 tablespoons balsamic vinegar
2 teaspoons dark brown sugar
1½lb rabbit
1 tablespoon olive oil
½ cup grated fresh Parmesan cheese
1 egg yolk
56 x 3½ inch square egg
  pastry sheets
1 egg, lightly beaten
all-purpose flour
⅔ cup grated fresh Parmesan
  cheese, extra

Melt butter in pan, add onions and carrot, cook, stirring, until onions are soft. Add vinegar and sugar, cook slowly, uncovered, about 40 minutes, stirring occasionally, until onions are golden brown. Remove onions from pan; cool.

Remove meat from rabbit; chop meat. Heat oil in pan, add rabbit, cook, stirring, until well browned and cooked; cool. Blend or process cheese, egg yolk, onion mixture and rabbit until finely chopped; cover, refrigerate until cold.

Top each pastry sheet with 2 level teaspoons of rabbit mixture. Brush edges of sheets with egg, fold sheets in half, press edges together to seal. Lightly sprinkle ravioli with flour.

Just before serving, add ravioli to large pan of boiling water, boil, uncovered, about 5 minutes or until just tender; drain. Serve with extra cheese.

Serves 8.

■ Ravioli can be made a day ahead.
■ Storage: Covered, in refrigerator.
■ Freeze: Uncooked ravioli suitable.
■ Microwave: Not suitable.

SPICY CHICKEN STIR-FRY WITH EGG NOODLES

½lb dried egg noodles
2 tablespoons oil
1¼lb chicken thighs, boned, skinned
2 cloves garlic, minced
½ teaspoon five-spice powder
½ teaspoon ground cumin
½ teaspoon curry powder
1 small fresh red chili pepper, chopped
1 red bell pepper, chopped
1 tablespoon Oriental sesame oil
3 tablespoons light soy sauce

Add noodles to pan of boiling water, boil, uncovered, until just tender; drain. Add half the oil to noodles, toss gently.

Cut chicken into thin strips. Heat remaining oil in wok or pan, add garlic, spices, chili pepper and chicken, stir-fry for about 5 minutes or until chicken is almost cooked. Stir in bell pepper, stir-fry 1 minute, stir in noodles, sesame oil and sauce, stir-fry until heated through.

Serves 4.

■ Recipe best made close to serving.
■ Freeze: Not suitable.
■ Microwave: Noodles suitable.

CHICKEN CANNELLONI WITH SHRIMP SAUCE

3 tablespoons butter
¼ cup all-purpose flour
1 cup water
1 small chicken bouillon cube, crumbled
1 tablespoon seeded mustard
¾ cup frozen green peas
2 cups (10oz) finely chopped cooked chicken
12 cannelloni pasta
all-purpose flour, extra
1 egg, lightly beaten
packaged unseasoned bread crumbs
oil for deep-frying

SHRIMP SAUCE
3 tablespoons butter
2 tablespoons all-purpose flour
2 teaspoons tomato paste
¼ cup dry red wine
1½ cups water
1 small chicken bouillon cube, crumbled
1 green onion, finely chopped
12 uncooked jumbo shrimp, shelled
2 tablespoons chopped fresh thyme

Melt butter in pan, add flour, stir over heat until lightly browned. Remove from heat, gradually stir in combined water, bouillon cube and mustard, bring to boil. Stir in peas, simmer, uncovered, for 2 minutes. Stir in chicken; cool.

Add pasta to large pan of boiling water, boil, uncovered, until just tender; drain.

Spoon chicken mixture into piping bag fitted with ¾ inch plain tube, pipe mixture into pasta. Roll pasta lightly in extra flour, dip in egg, then bread crumbs. Place pasta on tray; cover, refrigerate 20 minutes.

Just before serving, deep-fry pasta in batches in hot oil until well browned; drain on absorbent paper. Serve with hot sauce.

Shrimp Sauce: Melt butter in pan, add flour, stir over heat until bubbling. Remove from heat, gradually stir in paste, wine, water and bouillon cube. Stir over heat until mixture boils and thickens, simmer, uncovered, for 5 minutes. Stir in onion and shrimp, simmer further 5 minutes or until shrimp are cooked; stir in thyme.

Serves 6.

■ Recipe can be prepared a day ahead.
■ Storage: Covered, in refrigerator.
■ Freeze: Not suitable.
■ Microwave: Pasta suitable.

ABOVE LEFT: Clockwise from back: Spicy Chicken Stir-Fry with Egg Noodles, Onion and Rabbit Ravioli with Fresh Parmesan, Duck and Pasta Souffles.
RIGHT: Chicken Cannelloni with Shrimp Sauce.

CHICKEN WITH HERBED LEMON SAUCE

¾lb lasagnette pasta
¼ cup (½ stick) butter
1 teaspoon grated lemon zest
¼ cup lemon juice
1¼ cups heavy cream
3 tablespoons chopped
   fresh chives
2 tablespoons chopped
   fresh thyme
3 cups (15oz) chopped
   cooked chicken
½ cup grated fresh Parmesan cheese

Add pasta to large pan of boiling water, boil, uncovered, until just tender; drain.

Heat butter, zest and juice in pan until butter is melted. Add cream, half the herbs, chicken and pasta, stir until heated through. Serve sprinkled with remaining herbs and cheese.

Serves 4.

■ Recipe best made just before serving.
■ Freeze: Not suitable.
■ Microwave: Pasta suitable.

PEPPERED CHICKEN AND PASTA SALAD

3½oz penne pasta
1 cup (5oz) chopped
   cooked chicken
1 red onion, thinly sliced
1 apple, chopped
2 stalks celery, chopped

DRESSING
1 tablespoon drained green
   peppercorns, crushed
⅓ cup heavy cream
¼ cup mayonnaise
½ teaspoon grated lemon zest
2 tablespoons lemon juice
¼ teaspoon sugar

Add pasta to large pan of boiling water, boil, uncovered, until just tender; drain. Rinse pasta under cold water; drain.

Combine pasta, chicken, onion, apple and celery in bowl. Add dressing to pasta mixture, toss well.

Dressing: Combine all ingredients in bowl; mix well.

Serves 4.

■ Salad can be made a day ahead.
■ Storage: Covered, in refrigerator.
■ Freeze: Not suitable.
■ Microwave: Pasta suitable.

CHICKEN AND NOODLE PATTIES

¼ cup Chinese dried mushrooms
¼ cup vegetable oil
1 large onion, finely chopped
1 clove garlic, minced
7oz fresh fine egg noodles
4 eggs, lightly beaten
2 teaspoons rice vinegar
1 cup (7oz) finely chopped
   cooked chicken
3 green onions, chopped
3 tablespoons chopped
   fresh parsley
3 tablespoons cornstarch
1 teaspoon Oriental sesame oil

ORANGE SAUCE
¼ cup hoisin sauce
2 tablespoons oyster-flavored sauce
2 teaspoons grated orange zest
¼ cup fresh orange juice
2 teaspoons sugar
3 tablespoons water
¼ teaspoon cornstarch
1 tablespoon water, extra

Place mushrooms in bowl, cover with boiling water, stand 20 minutes. Drain mushrooms, discard liquid. Discard stems, slice caps thinly.

Heat 1 tablespoon of the oil in pan, add onion and garlic, cook, stirring, until onion is soft; cool. Combine onion mixture, mushrooms, noodles, eggs, vinegar, chicken, onions, parsley, cornstarch and sesame oil in bowl.

Shape ⅓ cup of mixture into a patty, repeat with remaining mixture. Heat remaining oil in pan, add patties, cook until lightly browned on both sides. Serve hot patties with warm sauce.

Orange Sauce: Combine sauces, zest, juice, sugar and water in pan, bring to boil. Stir in blended cornstarch and extra water, stir until sauce boils and thickens.

Serves 4.

■ Patties and sauce can be made
   a day ahead.
■ Storage: Covered, in refrigerator.
■ Freeze: Not suitable.
■ Microwave: Sauce suitable.

LEFT: Clockwise from left: Chicken and Noodle Patties, Chicken with Herbed Lemon Sauce, Peppered Chicken and Pasta Salad.

SEAFOOD

Fresh seafood is wonderful to cook with because it is usually quick and always popular. Lobster, shrimp, mussels, smoked salmon and all your favorites are here in dishes ranging from light and pretty to quite hearty eating (depending on the size of the helping, of course!). Even if you think you "can't cook" you'll find something here that is well within your skills. Again, lovely sauces are important and, in every dish, pasta is seafood's perfect partner, ready to star or be an accompaniment.

GARLIC CREAM MUSSELS WITH RIGATONI

¾lb rigatoni pasta
2lb mussels
3 tablespoons butter
1 onion, chopped
3 cloves garlic, minced
2 red bell peppers, chopped
½ cup sour cream
¼ cup dry white wine
4 green onions, finely chopped
3 tablespoons chopped fresh parsley

Add pasta to large pan of boiling water, boil, uncovered, until just tender; drain.

Scrub mussels, remove beards. Melt butter in large pan, add onion, cook, stirring, until soft. Add garlic and peppers, cook, stirring, for 2 minutes. Stir in sour cream and wine, bring to boil. Add mussels, bring to boil, simmer, covered, about 3 minutes or until shells have opened. Add green onions, parsley and pasta to pan, stir until just heated through.

Serves 6.

■ Recipe best made close to serving.
■ Freeze: Not suitable.
■ Microwave: Suitable.

SALMON CANNELLONI WITH PIMIENTO MINT SAUCE

1½ x 15oz cans salmon, drained
6oz feta cheese, crumbled
2 stalks celery, chopped
6 green onions, chopped
⅓ cup mayonnaise
2 tablespoons lemon juice
12 cannelloni pasta
¼ cup grated fresh Parmesan cheese

PIMIENTO MINT SAUCE
14½oz can tomatoes
6oz can pimientos, drained, chopped
1 cup fresh mint leaves
1 tablespoon dark brown sugar

Remove skin and bones from salmon. Combine salmon, feta cheese, celery, onions, mayonnaise and juice in bowl; mix well.

Add cannelloni to large pan of boiling water, boil, uncovered, until just tender; drain.

Spoon salmon mixture into cannelloni, place in greased ovenproof dish in single layer, cover, bake in 350°F oven about 15 minutes or until heated through. Serve cannelloni with hot sauce, sprinkle with Parmesan cheese.

Pimiento Mint Sauce: Combine undrained crushed tomatoes, pimientos, mint and sugar in pan. Bring to boil, simmer, uncovered, about 5 minutes or until mixture is reduced and thickened. Blend or process sauce until smooth.

Serves 4.

■ Recipe can be made a day ahead.
■ Storage: Covered, in refrigerator.
■ Freeze: Not suitable.
■ Microwave: Suitable.

FRESH TUNA CHUNKS IN HOT CHILI DRESSING

1lb piece fresh tuna
2 bay leaves
½ cup olive oil
3 tablespoons lemon juice
1 clove garlic, finely chopped
1 teaspoon cracked black peppercorns
2 tablespoons chopped fresh flat-leafed parsley
1 tablespoon butter
1 onion, thinly sliced
1 small fresh red chili pepper, shredded
1lb linguine pasta

Cut tuna into ¾ inch pieces, place into ovenproof dish with combined bay leaves, oil, juice, garlic, peppercorns and parsley; do not stir. Cover dish, bake in 350°F oven about 20 minutes or until tuna is cooked; discard bay leaves.

Melt butter in pan, add onion, cook, stirring, until soft. Stir in chili and tuna mixture, stir gently until heated through.

Add pasta to large pan of boiling water, boil, uncovered, until just tender; drain. Serve pasta with tuna mixture.

Serves 4.

■ Best made just before serving.
■ Freeze: Not suitable.
■ Microwave: Suitable.

RIGHT: Clockwise from left: Fresh Tuna Chunks in Hot Chili Dressing, Salmon Cannelloni with Pimiento Mint Sauce, Garlic Cream Mussels with Rigatoni.

HONEYED SCALLOPS WITH TROPICAL FRUIT SALSA

1lb sea scallops
1/3 cup honey
2 teaspoons chili sauce
1/2 cup dry white wine
1 teaspoon grated fresh gingerroot
1/2lb bow-tie pasta
1 tablespoon cornstarch
2 tablespoons water

TROPICAL FRUIT SALSA
1 1/2 cups (9oz) chopped fresh
    pineapple
1 cup (7oz) chopped fresh mango
1 tablespoon chopped fresh mint

Thread scallops onto small skewers, place in shallow glass dish. Pour combined honey, sauce, wine and gingerroot over kabobs; cover, refrigerate several hours. Drain kabobs, reserve marinade.
Just before serving, broil or barbeque kabobs until scallops are just cooked.

Add pasta to large pan of boiling water, boil, uncovered, until just tender; drain, keep warm.

Combine blended cornstarch and water with reserved marinade in pan, stir over heat until mixture boils and thickens.

Serve kabobs on pasta with thickened marinade, serve with tropical fruit salsa.
Tropical Fruit Salsa: Combine all ingredients in bowl; mix gently.
Serves 4.

■ Recipe can be prepared a day ahead.
■ Storage: Covered, in refrigerator.
■ Freeze: Not suitable.
■ Microwave: Pasta suitable.

LEMONY SEAFOOD IN SAFFRON GARLIC SAUCE

2lb mussels
1lb uncooked jumbo shrimp
1/2 cup dry white wine
1/2 cup water
1 lemon
tiny pinch saffron powder
1/2lb fettuccine pasta
1 tablespoon butter
1 tablespoon olive oil
2 cloves garlic, minced
2 green onions, chopped
1/2 cup heavy cream
2 egg yolks
2 tablespoons lemon juice
1 tablespoon chopped fresh oregano

Scrub mussels, remove beards. Shell and devein shrimp, leaving tails intact. Combine mussels, wine and water in pan, cover, bring to boil, simmer 1 minute. Strain mussels, reserve liquid.

Thinly cut peel from lemon. Combine peel in pan with reserved liquid and saffron, simmer, uncovered, until liquid is reduced by half. Strain, reserve liquid.

Add pasta to large pan of boiling water, boil, uncovered, until just tender; drain.

Heat butter and oil in pan, add garlic and onions, cook, stirring, 1 minute. Stir in reserved liquid and combined cream and egg yolks, stir, without boiling, until slightly thickened. Stir in seafood, juice and oregano, simmer, covered, about 2 minutes or until shrimp are cooked. Serve sauce over pasta.
Serves 4.

■ Sauce can be made a day ahead.
■ Storage: Covered, in refrigerator.
■ Freeze: Not suitable.
■ Microwave: Pasta suitable.

TOMATO, ANCHOVY AND ARTICHOKE SALAD

1lb pasta twists
4 large (2lb) tomatoes, peeled,
    seeded, chopped
1 cup (6oz) pitted black olives, halved
8oz jar artichoke hearts,
    drained, halved
2oz can anchovy fillets, drained,
    chopped

DRESSING
1/4 cup olive oil
1/4 cup lemon juice
1/4 cup chopped fresh basil
3 tablespoons chopped fresh parsley

Add pasta to large pan of boiling water, boil, uncovered, until just tender; drain.

Combine tomatoes, olives, artichokes, anchovies and pasta in bowl, add dressing; toss well.
Dressing: Combine all ingredients in jar; shake well.
Serves 4.

■ Salad can be made a day ahead.
■ Storage: Covered, in refrigerator.
■ Freeze: Not suitable.
■ Microwave: Pasta suitable.

LEFT: From left: Lemony Seafood in Saffron Garlic Sauce, Tomato, Anchovy and Artichoke Salad.
BELOW: Honeyed Scallops with Tropical Fruit Salsa.

SMOKED SALMON TORTELLINI WITH HOT CABBAGE SALAD

1 quantity plain pasta dough
1 egg, lightly beaten

FILLING
1 tablespoon olive oil
1 small onion, chopped
6oz smoked salmon pieces, chopped
2 tablespoons chopped
    fresh parsley

HOT CABBAGE SALAD
¼ cup olive oil
2 cloves garlic, minced
1 red bell pepper, sliced
¼ medium cabbage, shredded
½ teaspoon ground black
    peppercorns

Roll dough until ⅛ inch thick, cut into 3 inch rounds. Brush rounds with egg, top each round with 1 level teaspoon of filling, fold rounds in half, press edges together to seal. Pinch points together.
Just before serving, add tortellini to large pan of boiling water, boil, uncovered, for about 8 minutes or until just tender; drain. Serve tortellini over cabbage salad.
Filling: Heat oil in pan, add onion, cook, stirring, until soft; cool. Combine onion, salmon and parsley in bowl.
Hot Cabbage Salad: Heat oil in pan, add garlic and pepper, cook, stirring, until pepper is soft. Add cabbage and peppercorns, cook, stirring, until cabbage is soft.
Serves 4.

■ Tortellini can be made a day ahead.
■ Storage: Covered, in refrigerator.
■ Freeze: Cooked tortellini suitable.
■ Microwave: Not suitable.

GINGERED SHRIMP AND PEA NOODLES

1½lb uncooked medium shrimp
2 stalks fresh lemon grass,
    finely chopped
1 teaspoon ground coriander
2 teaspoons ground gingerroot
7oz sugar snap peas
1lb fresh egg noodles
3 tablespoons vegetable oil

BUTTER SAUCE
1 teaspoon cornstarch
3 tablespoons water
⅓ cup sake
2 tablespoons lemon juice
1 teaspoon grated fresh gingerroot
3oz (¾ stick) butter

Shell and devein shrimp, leaving tails intact. Combine shrimp, lemon grass, coriander and gingerroot in bowl; cover, refrigerate 1 hour.
Boil, steam or microwave peas until just tender; drain. Cover noodles with boiling water, stand 5 minutes; drain.
Heat oil in wok or pan, add shrimp mixture, stir-fry until shrimp are cooked through. Add peas, noodles and butter sauce, stir until heated through.
Butter Sauce: Combine blended cornstarch and water with sake, juice and gingerroot in pan, stir over heat until mixture boils and thickens. Remove from heat, add butter, stir until melted.
Serves 4.

■ Best made just before serving.
■ Freeze: Not suitable.
■ Microwave: Sauce suitable.

LEFT: From left: Gingered Shrimp and Pea Noodles, Smoked Salmon Tortellini with Hot Cabbage Salad.

QUICK SEAFOOD SHELLS

24 extra large pasta shells
1 tablespoon olive oil
1 onion, finely chopped
1 large (about 6oz) carrot, coarsely grated
1 large (about 7oz) zucchini, coarsely grated
3oz button mushrooms, finely chopped
2 tomatoes, finely chopped
¼ cup dry white wine
12½oz can tuna, drained, mashed
2oz can anchovies, drained, chopped
1 cup water
1 small chicken bouillon cube, crumbled
1½oz packaged cream cheese, chopped
2 tablespoons chopped fresh basil

Add pasta to large pan of boiling water, boil, uncovered, until just tender; drain.

Heat oil in pan, add onion, cook, stirring, until soft. Add carrot, zucchini and mushrooms, cook, stirring, until vegetables are soft. Stir in tomatoes and wine, simmer, uncovered, about 5 minutes or until mixture is slightly thickened.

Combine half the vegetable mixture with tuna and anchovies in bowl, spoon into pasta shells, place shells in greased ovenproof dish.
Just before serving, bake filled shells, covered, in 350°F oven about 10 minutes or until heated through.

Blend or process remaining vegetable mixture, water, bouillon cube and cream cheese until smooth. Pour mixture into pan, stir over heat until heated through; stir in basil. Serve sauce with shells.

Serves 4.

■ Recipe can be prepared a day ahead.
■ Storage: Covered, in refrigerator.
■ Freeze: Not suitable.
■ Microwave: Suitable.

PASTA MARINARA

2 tablespoons (¼ stick) butter
1 onion, chopped
1 clove garlic, minced
14½oz can tomatoes
3 tablespoons tomato paste
1 cup water
1 small chicken bouillon cube, crumbled
¾lb paglia e fieno pasta
1lb seafood marinara mix
3 tablespoons chopped fresh parsley
¼ cup grated fresh Parmesan cheese

Melt butter in pan, add onion and garlic, cook, stirring, until onion is soft. Add undrained crushed tomatoes, paste, water and bouillon cube. Bring to boil, simmer, uncovered, about 10 minutes or until sauce is thickened.

Add pasta to large pan of boiling water, boil, uncovered, until just cooked; drain.

Add marinara mix to sauce, simmer, uncovered, until seafood is cooked. Remove from heat, stir in parsley and cheese. Serve sauce over pasta.

Serves 4.

■ Recipe best made close to serving.
■ Freeze: Not suitable.
■ Microwave: Suitable.

CRAB RAVIOLI WITH TOMATO AND BELL PEPPER SAUCE

2 tablespoons olive oil
6 green onions, chopped
7oz white fish fillets
6oz can crab meat, drained, flaked
2 tablespoons lemon juice
1 tablespoon chopped fresh oregano
¼ cup packaged, unseasoned bread crumbs
2 egg yolks
60 x 3½in square wonton skins
1 egg, lightly beaten
½ cup grated fresh Parmesan cheese

TOMATO AND BELL PEPPER SAUCE
1 red bell pepper
2 tablespoons olive oil
1 clove garlic, minced
2 x 14½oz cans tomatoes
¼ teaspoon sugar
½ teaspoon grated orange zest

SMOKED TROUT AND HONEYDEW SALAD

1½ bunches (¾lb) fresh asparagus
7oz sliced smoked trout
1 cup (¼lb) mini bow-tie pasta
½ honeydew melon, sliced
1 Boston lettuce, shredded

STRAWBERRY VINAIGRETTE
¼lb strawberries
½ cup olive oil
¼ cup white vinegar
½ teaspoon sugar
¼ teaspoon ground black peppercorns

Boil, steam or microwave asparagus until just tender; drain. Place asparagus in bowl of iced water until cold; drain. Roll trout slices around asparagus.

Add pasta to large pan of boiling water, boil, uncovered, until just tender, drain; rinse under cold water, drain.

Just before serving, place melon, lettuce, pasta and trout rolls on plates, drizzle with vinaigrette.

Strawberry Vinaigrette: Blend or process strawberries until smooth, strain. Combine pureed strawberries with remaining ingredients in jar; shake well.

Serves 4 to 6.

■ Can be prepared 3 hours ahead.
■ Storage: Covered, in refrigerator.
■ Freeze: Not suitable.
■ Microwave: Suitable.

LEFT: Clockwise from left: Quick Seafood Shells, Pasta Marinara, Crab Ravioli with Tomato and Bell Pepper Sauce.
BELOW: Smoked Trout and Honeydew Salad.

Heat oil in pan, add onions, cook, stirring, until just soft. Add fish, cook, covered, turning once, until cooked. Mash fish in bowl; cool. Add crab, juice, oregano, bread crumbs and egg yolks to fish, mix well; cover, refrigerate 1 hour.

Top half the wonton skins with 2 level teaspoons of crab mixture, brush edges of skins with egg, top with remaining skins, press edges together to seal.

Just before serving, add ravioli to large pan of boiling water, boil, uncovered, about 6 minutes or until just tender; drain. Serve ravioli with warm sauce, sprinkled with Parmesan cheese.

Tomato and Bell Pepper Sauce: Cut pepper into quarters, remove seeds and membrane. Broil pepper, skin-side-up, until skin blackens and blisters. Peel skin, chop pepper.

Heat oil in pan, add pepper and garlic, cook, stirring, until pepper is soft. Stir in undrained crushed tomatoes and sugar, bring to boil, simmer, uncovered, about 5 minutes or until thickened. Blend or process mixture until smooth, stir in zest.

Serves 6.

■ Ravioli and sauce can be made a day ahead.
■ Storage: Covered, in refrigerator.
■ Freeze: Uncooked ravioli suitable.
■ Microwave: Not suitable.

SPICY FISH WITH OLIVES AND SUN-DRIED TOMATOES

¼ cup olive oil
1 onion, thinly sliced
2 cloves garlic, sliced
2 tablespoons chopped drained
    anchovy fillets
2 tablespoons chopped
    drained capers
2 teaspoons sambal oelek
¼ cup chopped drained sun-dried
    tomatoes
1lb white fish fillets, chopped
½ cup black olives
¾lb tomato tagliatelle pasta

Heat oil in pan, add onion and garlic, cook, stirring, until onion is soft. Stir in anchovies, capers, sambal oelek and tomatoes. Add fish to pan, cook over low heat until cooked; add olives.

Add pasta to large pan of boiling water, boil, uncovered, until just tender; drain. Serve pasta with fish mixture.

Serves 4.

■ Recipe best made close to serving.
■ Freeze: Not suitable.
■ Microwave: Suitable.

SMOKED SALMON POUCHES WITH PIMIENTO CREAM

3½oz smoked salmon pieces,
    finely chopped
3oz packaged cream cheese,
    softened
1 tablespoon finely chopped
    drained pimientos
2 tablespoons lemon juice
2 tablespoons chopped fresh chives
½lb packet gow gees pastry

PIMIENTO CREAM
3 tablespoons chopped
    drained pimientos
1 teaspoon lemon juice
2 teaspoons chopped fresh dill
½ cup heavy cream

Combine salmon, cheese, pimientos, juice and chives in bowl. Top each pastry sheet with 1 level teaspoon of salmon mixture. Brush edges of pastry lightly with water, gather edges together around salmon mixture to form pouches.

Just before serving, add pouches to large pan of boiling water, boil, uncovered, about 3 minutes or until just tender; drain. Serve pouches with pimiento cream and extra dill, if desired.

Pimiento Cream: Blend or process all ingredients until almost smooth. Transfer mixture to pan, stir over low heat until heated through.

Serves 4.

■ Can be prepared a day ahead.
■ Storage: Covered, in refrigerator.
■ Freeze: Uncooked pouches suitable.
■ Microwave: Pimiento cream suitable.

TOMATO AND SHRIMP PASTA BAKES

1lb vegetable pasta twists
2 tablespoons olive oil
¼ cup (½ stick) butter
2 leeks, sliced
4 cloves garlic, minced
1 teaspoon chili powder
2 tablespoons chopped fresh oregano
2 x 14½oz cans tomatoes
¼ cup dry sherry
2lb uncooked shrimp,
    shelled, chopped
7oz feta cheese, crumbled

Add pasta to large pan of boiling water, boil, uncovered, until just tender; drain.

Heat oil and butter in pan, add leeks, garlic and chili, cook, stirring, until leeks are soft. Stir in oregano, undrained, crushed tomatoes, sherry and shrimp, bring to boil, simmer 1 minute. Spoon pasta into 6 greased ovenproof dishes (2 cup capacity), top with shrimp mixture, sprinkle with cheese.

Just before serving, bake in 375°F oven about 10 minutes or until cheese is browned and pasta heated through.

Serves 6.

■ Can be prepared a day ahead.
■ Storage: Covered, in refrigerator.
■ Freeze: Not suitable.
■ Microwave: Pasta suitable.

RIGHT: Clockwise from back: Smoked Salmon Pouches with Pimiento Cream, Spicy Fish with Olives and Sun-Dried Tomatoes, Tomato and Shrimp Pasta Bakes.

FIVE SEAFOODS WITH FENNEL CREAM SAUCE

4 large (about 6oz) cooked jumbo
    shrimp
2 tablespoons (¼ stick) butter
1 onion, chopped
1 clove garlic, minced
3 tablespoons all-purpose flour
2 cups milk
1¼ cups heavy cream
1 teaspoon fennel seeds, crushed
7oz white fish fillets, chopped
7oz salmon fillet, chopped
5oz sea scallops
5oz mussel meat
¾lb spinach fettuccine pasta
3 green onions, chopped

Shell and devein shrimp, leaving heads
and tails intact. Melt butter in pan, add
onion and garlic, cook, stirring, until onion
is soft. Stir in flour, cook until bubbling.
Remove from heat, gradually stir in milk,
cream and seeds. Stir over heat until
sauce boils and thickens slightly. Stir in
seafood, simmer, uncovered, about 5
minutes or until seafood is cooked.

Add pasta to large pan of boiling water,
boil, uncovered, until just tender; drain.
Serve fennel cream sauce over pasta,
sprinkle with green onions.

Serves 4.

■ Recipe best made just before serving.
■ Freeze: Not suitable.
■ Microwave: Suitable.

STIR-FRIED SEAFOOD SALAD

2 tablespoons honey
1 tablespoon light soy sauce
1 tablespoon oyster-flavored sauce
1 tablespoon dry sherry
1 teaspoon Oriental sesame oil
2 teaspoons grated fresh gingerroot
1 clove garlic, minced
¾lb uncooked jumbo shrimp, shelled
½lb cleaned squid hoods, sliced
½lb fresh egg noodles
2 tablespoons oil
4 green onions, chopped
1 red bell pepper, sliced
8oz can sliced bamboo
    shoots, drained

Combine honey, sauces, sherry, oil, gingerroot, garlic, shrimp and squid in bowl; cover,
refrigerate 3 hours or overnight.

Add noodles to large pan of boiling
water, boil, uncovered, until just tender;
drain, rinse under cold water; drain.

Remove seafood from marinade,
reserve marinade. Heat oil in wok or pan,
add onions, pepper and bamboo shoots,
stir over heat 1 minute; add seafood, stir-
fry until just cooked.

Stir in noodles and reserved marinade;
stir until mixture is heated through.
Remove from heat, cool; cover, refrigerate
for 2 hours before serving.

Serves 6.

■ Salad can be made a day ahead.
■ Storage: Covered, in refrigerator.
■ Freeze: Not suitable.
■ Microwave: Noodles suitable.

SMOKED TROUT WITH BUTTERED HERB PASTA

¾lb sliced smoked ocean trout
¼lb cherry tomatoes
⅓ cup sliced pitted black olives
1 teaspoon chopped fresh dill
1 tablespoon sugar
3 tablespoons lime juice
1½ teaspoons French mustard
⅓ cup olive oil

BUTTERED HERB PASTA
1½ cups all-purpose flour
¼ cup fine semolina
¼ cup cornmeal
3 eggs
1 tablespoon chopped fresh mint
1 tablespoon chopped fresh dill
1 tablespoon chopped fresh basil
3oz (¾ stick) unsalted butter
2 tablespoons chopped fresh
    basil, extra
2 teaspoons chopped fresh
    mint, extra

Cut trout into thin strips, combine with
tomatoes, olives and dill in bowl. Pour
over combined sugar, juice, mustard and
oil; cover, refrigerate 2 hours, stirring
occasionally. Serve trout mixture with
warm pasta.

Buttered Herb Pasta: Process flour,
semolina, cornmeal, eggs and herbs until
mixture forms a ball; cover with plastic
wrap, stand 2 hours.

Knead dough until smooth, roll until ⅛
inch thick, cut into thin strips using pasta
machine. Add pasta to large pan of boiling
water, boil, uncovered, about 2 minutes or
until just tender; drain.

Heat butter in pan, add extra herbs and pasta, stir gently until combined.

Serves 6.

■ Recipe can be prepared a day ahead.
■ Storage: Covered, in refrigerator.
■ Freeze: Not suitable.
■ Microwave: Pasta suitable.

CRAB AND NOODLE SALAD WITH LEMON DRESSING

10oz fresh egg noodles
1 stalk celery
1 apple, chopped
1 tablespoon lemon juice
2 tablespoons chopped fresh dill
2 x 6oz cans crab meat,
**   drained, flaked**

LEMON DRESSING
1 teaspoon French mustard
1 teaspoon sugar
1 tablespoon white vinegar
2 tablespoons lemon juice
2 tablespoons olive oil

Add noodles to large pan of boiling water, boil, uncovered, until just tender; drain. Rinse noodles under cold water; drain.

Cut celery into 2 inch sticks. Combine celery, apple, juice, dill, crab, noodles and dressing in bowl; mix well.

Lemon Dressing: Combine all ingredients in jar; shake well.

Serves 6.

■ Salad can be made a day ahead.
■ Storage: Covered, in refrigerator.
■ Freeze: Not suitable.
■ Microwave: Noodles suitable.

LEFT: Five Seafoods with Fennel Cream Sauce.
ABOVE: Clockwise from front: Smoked Trout with Buttered Herb Pasta, Crab and Noodle Salad with Lemon Dressing, Stir-Fried Seafood Salad.

53

SMOKED SALMON WITH FRESH ASPARAGUS

1lb spaghetti pasta
¾lb sliced smoked salmon
2 tablespoons olive oil
1 onion, chopped
2 bunches (1lb) fresh asparagus,
   chopped
1 tablespoon brandy
2 teaspoons white mustard seeds
2½ cups heavy cream
3 tablespoons shredded fresh basil

Add pasta to large pan of boiling water, boil, uncovered, until just tender, drain.

Cut salmon into ¾ inch strips. Heat oil in pan, add onion, cook, stirring, until soft. Add salmon, asparagus, brandy, seeds and cream. Simmer, uncovered, until slightly thickened; stir in basil. Serve hot sauce over pasta.

Serves 4.

■ Recipe best made just before serving.
■ Freeze: Not suitable.
■ Microwave: Suitable.

LEFT: From back: Eggplant and Anchovy Pasta, Smoked Salmon with Fresh Asparagus.
BELOW: Spinach Fettuccine with Shrimp and Artichokes.

EGGPLANT AND ANCHOVY PASTA

¾lb penne pasta
1 medium (about 10oz) eggplant
4 medium (about 13oz) zucchini
2 tablespoons olive oil
1 clove garlic, minced
1 small fresh red chili pepper,
   finely chopped
1 onion, chopped
2oz can anchovy fillets,
   drained, chopped
¼ cup (½ stick) butter

Add pasta to large pan of boiling water, boil, uncovered, until just tender, drain.

Cut eggplant and zucchini into 2 inch strips. Heat oil in pan, add garlic, chili and onion, cook, stirring, until onion is soft. Add eggplant and zucchini, cook, stirring, until tender. Stir in anchovies and butter, stir until butter is melted. Add pasta, stir until heated through.

Serves 4.

■ Recipe best made close to serving.
■ Freeze: Not suitable.
■ Microwave: Pasta suitable.

SPINACH FETTUCCINE WITH SHRIMP AND ARTICHOKES

1lb cooked jumbo shrimp
¼ cup olive oil
2 cloves garlic, minced
1 small onion, chopped
1 red bell pepper, chopped
2 x 14½oz cans tomatoes
1 tablespoon chopped fresh chives
3 tablespoons chopped fresh basil
7oz jar artichoke hearts,
   drained, halved
1lb spinach fettuccine pasta
3½oz feta cheese, crumbled

Shell and devein shrimp, leaving tails intact. Heat oil in pan, add garlic, onion and pepper, cook, stirring, until onion and pepper are soft. Stir in undrained crushed tomatoes, simmer, uncovered, about 5 minutes or until slightly thickened. Stir in herbs, artichokes and shrimp, cook until heated through.

Add pasta to large pan of boiling water, boil, uncovered, until just tender; drain. Serve hot pasta with hot sauce, topped with cheese.

Serves 4.

■ Recipe best made close to serving.
■ Freeze: Not suitable.
■ Microwave: Pasta suitable.

CHEESY SALMON LASAGNE

2 tablespoons (¼ stick) butter
2 onions, chopped
1 clove garlic, minced
1 stalk celery, chopped
2 x 14½oz cans tomatoes
2 tablespoons tomato paste
15oz can salmon, drained, flaked
½lb packaged instant lasagne
    pasta sheets
1 tablespoon grated Parmesan
    cheese

CHEESE SAUCE
¼ cup (½ stick) butter
¼ cup all-purpose flour
1 cup milk
½lb cottage cheese
½ cup grated cheddar cheese
2 eggs, lightly beaten

Heat butter in pan, add onions, garlic and celery; cook, stirring, until onions are soft. Stir in undrained crushed tomatoes and paste, bring to boil, simmer, uncovered, 15 minutes; stir in salmon.

Cover base of greased 8 inch x 12 inch ovenproof dish with a layer of pasta. Spread pasta with half the salmon mixture, then half the cheese sauce; repeat layers ending with cheese sauce; sprinkle with Parmesan cheese. Bake lasagne in 350°F oven about 45 minutes or until lightly browned.

Cheese Sauce: Melt butter in pan, stir in flour, stir over heat until bubbling. Remove from heat, gradually stir in milk, stir over heat until sauce boils and thickens. Remove sauce from heat, stir in cheeses and eggs.

Serves 6.

■ Recipe can be made a day ahead.
■ Storage: Covered, in refrigerator.
■ Freeze: Not suitable.
■ Microwave: Not suitable.

ORANGE AND SALMON PASTA SALAD

½lb bow-tie pasta
2 teaspoons olive oil
½lb salmon cutlet
2 green onions, chopped
2 oranges, segmented
1 stalk celery, chopped
½ cup pecans
3 cups (½lb) shredded red cabbage

DRESSING
¼ cup olive oil
2 tablespoons lemon juice
1 teaspoon light soy sauce
1 clove garlic, minced

Add pasta to large pan of boiling water, boil, uncovered, until just tender; drain.

Combine pasta and oil in bowl. Add salmon to shallow pan of simmering water, simmer, covered, about 5 minutes or until tender; cool. Remove skin and bones from salmon, break salmon into pieces.

Just before serving, combine pasta, salmon, onions, oranges, celery, nuts and cabbage in bowl; mix well. Add dressing, toss lightly.

Dressing: Combine all ingredients in jar; shake well.

Serves 4.

■ Salad can be made 3 hours ahead.
■ Storage: Covered, in refrigerator.
■ Freeze: Not suitable.
■ Microwave: Suitable.

SALMON AND ORZO BONBONS

½ cup all-purpose flour
2 teaspoons tomato paste
2 eggs, lightly beaten
¾ cup milk
16 long fresh chives
1 tablespoon butter, melted
2 tablespoons chopped fresh
    chives, extra
1 clove garlic, minced

FILLING
½ cup orzo pasta
7½oz can salmon, drained, mashed
3 tablespoons horseradish cream
1 green onion, finely chopped
2 tablespoons sour cream

Sift flour into bowl, gradually stir in combined paste, eggs and milk, beat until smooth (or blend or process all ingredients until smooth); cover, stand 30 minutes.

Pour 3 to 4 tablespoons of batter into heated greased heavy-based crepe pan, cook until lightly browned underneath. Turn crepe, brown on other side. Repeat with remaining batter. You will need 8 crepes for this recipe.

Divide filling along 1 side of each crepe, roll crepes firmly. Drop long chives into pan of boiling water; drain. Tie a chive around each end of bonbons. Place bonbons on lightly greased baking sheet, cover loosely with foil.

Just before serving, heat bonbons in 350°F oven about 10 minutes. Brush bonbons with combined butter, extra chives and garlic.

Filling: Add pasta to pan of boiling water, boil, uncovered, until just tender; drain. Combine pasta, salmon, horseradish, onion and sour cream in bowl.

Serves 4.

■ Bonbons can be made 2 days ahead.
■ Storage: Covered, in refrigerator.
■ Freeze: Unfilled crepes suitable.
■ Microwave: Pasta suitable.

LEFT: Salmon and Orzo Bonbons.
RIGHT: From back: Cheesy Salmon Lasagne, Orange and Salmon Pasta Salad.

SALMON CHUNKS IN CRISP CHAMPAGNE BATTER

5oz angels' hair pasta
1½ bunches (¾lb) fresh asparagus
1 tablespoon olive oil
1 clove garlic, minced
3 green onions, chopped
1 tablespoon light soy sauce

1¼ cups heavy cream
2 thick (1¼lb) salmon steaks
oil for deep-frying
¼ cup lemon juice

CHAMPAGNE BATTER
⅔ cup all-purpose flour
⅓ cup champagne
⅓ cup soda water

Add pasta to large pan of boiling water, boil, uncovered, until just tender; drain. Cut asparagus into 1¼ inch lengths. Heat olive oil in pan, add asparagus, garlic and onions, cook, stirring, 3 minutes. Remove from heat, stir in sauce. Bring cream to boil in separate pan, simmer, uncovered, about 4 minutes or until thickened slightly, stir into asparagus mixture. Cut salmon into bite-sized chunks.

Just before serving, dip salmon chunks in batter, deep-fry in hot oil until lightly browned and crisp; drain on absorbent paper. Combine hot pasta and sauce, fold in salmon, sprinkle with juice.

Champagne Batter: Sift flour into bowl, stir in champagne and soda water all at once, beat to a smooth batter.

Serves 4.

- Recipe can be prepared 6 hours ahead. Batter best made just before using.
- Storage: Covered, in refrigerator.
- Freeze: Not suitable.
- Microwave: Noodles suitable.

LOBSTER IN WINE AND PEPPERCORN GLAZE

2 uncooked lobster tails
all-purpose flour
2 tablespoons butter
2 tablespoons port wine
½ cup dry white wine
½ cup water
1 small chicken bouillon cube, crumbled
1 tablespoon drained green peppercorns
¼ cup heavy cream
¾lb twisted pasta sticks
2 tablespoons (¼ stick) butter, extra
2 tablespoons chopped fresh parsley

Remove lobster meat from shells in 1 piece; cut meat into ½ inch medallions. Toss lobster in flour, shake away excess flour. Heat butter in pan, add medallions in single layer, cook about 2 minutes on each side or until almost cooked. Add port, white wine, water, bouillon cube and peppercorns, simmer gently, covered, until medallions are cooked. Remove medallions from pan; keep warm.

Boil sauce, uncovered, about 3 minutes or until reduced to a shiny glaze, add cream, stir until heated through.

Add pasta to large pan of boiling water, boil, uncovered, until just tender; drain. Add extra butter to same pan, stir until melted and lightly browned, return pasta to pan with parsley, mix well. Serve pasta with lobster and sauce.

Serves 4.

- Recipe best made just before serving.
- Freeze: Not suitable.
- Microwave: Pasta suitable.

LEFT: From back: Salmon Chunks in Crisp Champagne Batter, Lobster in Wine and Peppercorn Glaze.

CRISPY FISH WITH LEEK AND NOODLES

¼ cup cornstarch
¼ teaspoon five-spice powder
1 egg, lightly beaten
1 teaspoon dark soy sauce
1lb white fish fillets
6 Chinese dried mushrooms
3 tablespoons butter
2 teaspoons grated fresh gingerroot
1 leek, thinly sliced
¼ cup roasted unsalted cashews
¼ cup oyster-flavored sauce
½lb fresh egg noodles
2 teaspoons Oriental sesame oil
1 tablespoon chopped fresh cilantro
oil for deep-frying
2 green onions, sliced

Sift cornstarch and spice into bowl, stir in egg and soy sauce, stir until smooth. Chop fish into ¾ inch cubes, add to cornstarch mixture, mix well; cover, refrigerate 1 hour.

Place mushrooms in bowl, cover with boiling water, stand 20 minutes. Drain mushrooms, discard liquid. Discard stems, slice caps thinly.

Melt butter in pan, add gingerroot and leek, cook, stirring, until leek is soft. Remove from heat, stir in cashews, oyster sauce and mushrooms; keep warm.

Place noodles in heatproof bowl, cover with boiling water, stand 5 minutes; drain. Add noodles to leek mixture, stir in sesame oil and cilantro; heat through.

Deep-fry fish pieces in batches in hot oil until well browned and cooked through; drain on absorbent paper. Serve fish over noodle mixture, sprinkle with onions.

Serves 4.

■ Fish can be prepared a day ahead.
■ Storage: Covered, in refrigerator.
■ Freeze: Not suitable.
■ Microwave: Not suitable.

SHRIMP AND CRAB CASSEROLE

¼lb ziti pasta
¼ cup (½ stick) butter
⅓ cup grated fresh Parmesan cheese

FILLING
3oz (¾ stick) butter
⅓ cup all-purpose flour
1½ cups milk
1 cup (2½oz) grated fresh
   Parmesan cheese
3oz cooked shelled shrimp, chopped
6oz can crab meat, drained, flaked
2 tablespoons chopped fresh chives
5 eggs, separated

Lightly grease 2½ inch deep ovenproof dish (8 cup capacity). Add pasta to large pan of boiling water, boil, uncovered, until just tender; drain. Return pasta to pan, stir butter and cheese through pasta; cool.

Cut pasta into 2 inch lengths, stand pasta around edge of prepared dish. Chop remaining pasta, combine with filling. Pour filling carefully into dish, bake in 375°F oven about 35 minutes or until set and well browned.

Filling: Melt butter in pan, stir in flour, stir over heat until bubbling. Remove from heat, gradually stir in milk, stir over heat until sauce boils and thickens; cool 5 minutes. Stir in cheese, shrimp, crab, chives and lightly beaten egg yolks. Beat egg whites in small bowl with electric mixer until soft peaks form, fold lightly into shrimp mixture.

Serves 6.

■ Recipe best made close to serving.
■ Freeze: Not suitable.
■ Microwave: Pasta and filling suitable.

BELOW: From left: Crispy Fish with Leek and Noodles, Shrimp and Crab Casserole.

BEEF

Expect the unexpected in this section, because we've been generous with assertive flavors to enhance the good robust taste of beef, so satisfyingly partnered by pasta.
Just to tempt you, there are tender cuts of steak and pastrami to serve in smart salads, in stir-fries with noodles, a curry or double-fried into crisp, spicy morsels. And there's ground beef, and lots of it, terrifically tasty in just over half the recipes.

WARM BEEF AND WALNUT SALAD

1lb pasta elbows
1lb piece beef tenderloin
3 tablespoons lemon juice
3 tablespoons light soy sauce
2 tablespoons oyster-flavored sauce
2 cloves garlic, minced
3 tablespoons olive oil
1 red bell pepper, chopped
1 cup (¼lb) chopped walnuts
4 green onions, chopped

DRESSING
¼ cup olive oil
1 clove garlic, minced
1 tablespoon white vinegar
1 tablespoon lemon juice
1 tablespoon chopped fresh chives

Add pasta to large pan of boiling water, boil, uncovered, until just tender, drain; keep warm.

Cut beef into ½ inch cubes, combine with juice, sauces and garlic in bowl; cover, refrigerate 1 hour.

Heat oil in pan, add beef mixture in batches, cook, stirring, until beef is cooked as desired. Combine beef mixture and pasta in bowl; keep warm.

Add pepper to pan of boiling water, boil 1 minute; drain. Add pepper, nuts, onions and dressing to pasta; toss well.
Dressing: Combine all ingredients in pan, stir over heat until heated through.

Serves 4.

■ Recipe best made just before serving.
■ Freeze: Not suitable.
■ Microwave: Pasta suitable.

PARSLEY MEATBALLS IN CREAMY CHEESE SAUCE

1lb ground beef
1 onion, finely chopped
1 egg, lightly beaten
¼ cup tomato paste
1 tablespoon Worcestershire sauce
¼ cup chopped fresh parsley
2 cups (2½ oz) fresh bread crumbs
all-purpose flour
oil for deep-frying
¾lb tagliatelle pasta
¼ cup (½ stick) butter
1¼ cups heavy cream
2 cups (5oz) grated fresh
    Parmesan cheese
¼ cup chopped fresh parsley, extra

Combine beef, onion, egg, paste, sauce, parsley and bread crumbs in bowl; mix well. Shape 1 tablespoon into a ball, toss lightly in flour; shake away excess flour. Repeat with remaining mixture.

Deep-fry meatballs in hot oil until well browned and cooked through, drain on absorbent paper; keep warm.

Add pasta to large pan of boiling water, boil, uncovered, until just tender; drain.

Melt butter in pan, stir in cream and cheese, stir, without boiling, until sauce is heated through. Remove sauce from heat, stir in extra parsley and meatballs, serve over pasta.

Serves 4.

■ Meatballs can be made a day ahead. Sauce best made close to serving.
■ Storage: Covered, in refrigerator.
■ Freeze: Meatballs suitable.
■ Microwave: Pasta suitable.

EASY BEEF RAVIOLI WITH LEMON DRESSING

1lb beef ravioli
3½oz button mushrooms, sliced
13oz can pimientos, drained, sliced
⅓ cup pitted black olives, sliced
⅓ cup small fresh oregano leaves

LEMON DRESSING
⅓ cup lemon juice
½ cup olive oil
1 clove garlic, minced
½ teaspoon sugar
¼ teaspoon seasoned pepper

Add ravioli to large pan of boiling water, boil, uncovered, until just tender; drain.

Combine ravioli, mushrooms, pimientos, olives and oregano in bowl; mix well. Pour over dressing; mix well.
Dressing: Combine all ingredients in jar; shake well.

Serves 4.

■ Can be made several hours ahead.
■ Storage: Covered, in refrigerator.
■ Freeze: Not suitable.
■ Microwave: Not suitable.

RIGHT: Clockwise from front: Warm Beef and Walnut Salad, Easy Beef Ravioli with Lemon Dressing, Parsley Meatballs in Creamy Cheese Sauce.

SPICY BEEF PIE WITH TOMATO SALSA

¼lb spaghettini pasta
2 eggs, lightly beaten
½ cup sour cream
1 cup (2½oz) grated fresh
  Parmesan cheese
1 tablespoon olive oil
1 onion, finely chopped
½lb ground beef
1oz sachet chili seasoning mix
1 tablespoon tomato paste
1 cup water
1 small chicken bouillon cube,
  crumbled
15oz can garbanzo beans, rinsed,
  drained

TOMATO SALSA
2 large tomatoes, finely chopped
2 green onions, chopped
½ teaspoon sugar
2 tablespoons lemon juice
2 tablespoons chopped fresh cilantro

Add pasta to large pan of boiling water, boil, uncovered, until just tender; drain.

Combine pasta, eggs, sour cream and half the cheese in bowl. Heat oil in pan, add onion, cook, stirring, until soft. Add beef, cook, stirring, until well browned. Stir in seasoning mix, paste, water and bouillon cube. Bring to boil, simmer, uncovered, 5 minutes. Stir in garbanzo beans, simmer, uncovered, further 5 minutes or until thickened.

Press half the pasta mixture over base and side of greased 9 inch pie dish. Spread with beef mixture, press firmly. Top with remaining pasta mixture, sprinkle with remaining cheese. Bake pie in 350°F oven about 1¼ hours or until well browned. Stand pie 5 minutes before cutting, serve with tomato salsa.
Tomato Salsa: Combine all ingredients in bowl; cover, stand 20 minutes.

Serves 6.

■ Recipe can be made a day ahead.
■ Storage: Covered, in refrigerator.
■ Freeze: Pie suitable.
■ Microwave: Pasta suitable.

PASTRAMI AND DILL SALAD

½lb radiatore pasta
3oz green beans, sliced
7oz sliced pastrami, chopped
3 dill pickles, sliced
¼lb cherry tomatoes

DRESSING
8oz carton sour cream
1 teaspoon grated orange zest
½ cup orange juice
¼ cup lemon juice
1 tablespoon seeded mustard
1 teaspoon chopped fresh dill

MEATBALLS IN STROGANOFF SAUCE

½lb ground beef
½lb ground pork
1 egg, lightly beaten
1 cup (2½oz) fresh bread crumbs
¼ cup tomato paste
¼ cup (½ stick) butter
2 onions, sliced
2 cloves garlic, minced
3 tablespoons all-purpose flour
2 cups water
1 small chicken bouillon cube,
  crumbled
¼ cup dry red wine
1lb fettuccine pasta
½lb mushrooms, chopped
¼ cup sour cream
2 tablespoons chopped fresh parsley

Combine beef, pork, egg, bread crumbs and paste in bowl; mix well. Shape 1 rounded tablespoon of mixture into a ball; repeat with remaining mixture.

Melt butter in pan, add meatballs in single layer, cook, shaking pan occasionally, until browned and cooked through; drain on absorbent paper.

Drain pan, leaving 3 tablespoons drippings in pan. Add onions and garlic to pan, cook, stirring, until onions are soft. Stir in flour, stir over heat until bubbling. Remove from heat, gradually stir in combined water, bouillon cube and wine, stir over heat until mixture boils and thickens.

Add pasta to large pan of boiling water, boil, uncovered, until just tender; drain.
Just before serving, combine mushrooms, sour cream, parsley and meatballs in pan, stir over heat until heated through, serve with pasta.

Serves 4.

■ Recipe can be made a day ahead.
■ Storage: Covered, in refrigerator.
■ Freeze: Cooked meatballs suitable.
■ Microwave: Pasta suitable.

LEFT: From left: Pastrami and Dill Salad, Meatballs in Stroganoff Sauce, Spicy Beef Pie with Tomato Salsa.

SPICY BEEF AND PASTA CASSEROLE

1lb whole-wheat pasta wheels
3 tablespoons olive oil
1 tablespoon bottled chopped chilies
2 cloves garlic, minced
2 red onions, sliced
1½lb ground beef
13oz can pimientos, drained, chopped   — *sweet Red Peppers*
2 x 14½oz cans tomatoes
1½ cups canned whole-kernel corn, drained
½ teaspoon cracked black peppercorns
½lb mozzarella cheese, shredded

Add pasta to large pan of boiling water, boil, uncovered, until just tender; drain.

Heat oil in pan, add chilies, garlic and onions, cook, stirring, until onions are soft. Add beef, cook, stirring, until well browned. Stir in pimientos, undrained crushed tomatoes, corn and peppercorns.

Spoon half the pasta into greased ovenproof dish (12 cup capacity). Top with half the beef mixture and half the cheese, continue layering, finishing with cheese. Bake, uncovered, in 350°F oven about 15 minutes or until heated through and cheese is melted.

Serves 8.

■ Recipe can be made a day ahead.
■ Storage: Covered, in refrigerator.
■ Freeze: Suitable.
■ Microwave: Pasta suitable.

BEEF AND BACON RAVIOLI WITH TERIYAKI SAUCE

¼lb ground beef
1 small onion, chopped
1 slice bacon, chopped
1 clove garlic, minced
2 tablespoons chopped fresh parsley
¼ teaspoon ground nutmeg
½lb packet wonton skins
1 egg white, lightly beaten

TERIYAKI SAUCE
3oz (¾ stick) unsalted butter
2 tablespoons all-purpose flour
1 cup water
¼ cup teriyaki marinade
⅓ cup green ginger wine
½ red bell pepper, thinly sliced
2 green onions, sliced

Blend or process beef, onion, bacon, garlic, parsley and nutmeg until smooth. Brush a wonton skin lightly with egg white, place ½ level teaspoon of filling on each quarter of skin. Top with a second skin, press between filling and on edges of skins to seal. Cut into quarters between

filling and trim edges using a pastry cutter. Repeat with remaining skins, egg white and filling.

Just before serving, add ravioli to large pan of boiling water, boil, uncovered, about 4 minutes or until just tender; drain. Serve ravioli with teriyaki sauce.

Teriyaki Sauce: Melt half of the butter in pan, stir in flour, stir over heat until bubbling. Remove from heat, gradually stir in combined water, marinade, wine and remaining butter. Stir over high heat until sauce boils and thickens, stir in pepper and onions, simmer 1 minute.

Serves 4.

■ Ravioli and sauce can be prepared 3 hours ahead.
■ Storage: Covered, in refrigerator.
■ Freeze: Uncooked ravioli suitable.
■ Microwave: Sauce suitable.

BEEF CURRY WITH YOGURT AND COCONUT CREAM

¼ cup olive oil
2 onions, sliced
2lb beef chuck, chopped
2 cloves garlic, minced
½ teaspoon ground cardamom
1 teaspoon ground cinnamon
1 teaspoon garam masala
2 tablespoons hot chili sauce
1 tablespoon sugar
⅔ cup canned unsweetened coconut cream
¾ cup plain yogurt
1 cup water
3 tablespoons lemon juice
2 small green cucumbers, sliced
¾lb pasta twists
1 teaspoon cuminseed
3 tablespoons chopped fresh cilantro

Heat oil in pan, add onions, cook, stirring, until soft. Add beef, cook, stirring, until well browned. Stir in garlic, spices, sauce, sugar, coconut cream, yogurt and water. Simmer, covered, about 1 hour or until beef is tender, stirring occasionally.

Remove cover, simmer, further 15 minutes or until slightly thickened. Stir in juice and cucumbers, remove from heat, stand covered, for 5 minutes.

Add pasta to large pan of boiling water, boil, uncovered, until just tender; drain. Combine pasta with cuminseed and cilantro, serve with curry.

Serves 6.

■ Curry can be made a day ahead.
■ Storage: Covered, in refrigerator.
■ Freeze: Curry suitable.
■ Microwave: Pasta suitable.

ABOVE LEFT: Spicy Beef and Pasta Casserole.
RIGHT: From left: Beef Curry with Yogurt and Coconut Cream, Beef and Bacon Ravioli with Teriyaki Sauce.

CHEESY SPAGHETTI AND BEEF SLICE

½ cup (1 stick) butter
1 cup all-purpose flour
4 cups milk
3 egg yolks
1¾ cups (5oz) finely grated
    kefalogravier (sheeps' milk) cheese
1lb spaghetti pasta
3oz (¾ stick) butter, extra
¼ cup fresh bread crumbs
¼ teaspoon ground nutmeg

MEAT SAUCE
¼ cup (½ stick) butter
2 onions, chopped
1 clove garlic, minced
2lb ground beef
4 large (about 1½lb) tomatoes,
    peeled, chopped
2 tablespoons tomato paste
2 teaspoons sugar
4 whole cloves
1 bay leaf
¼ teaspoon ground cinnamon
3 egg whites

Melt butter in pan, add flour, stir over heat until bubbling. Remove from heat, gradually stir in milk, stir over heat until mixture boils and thickens. Stir in egg yolks and ⅓ cup of the cheese; cool.

Add pasta to large pan of boiling water, boil, uncovered, until just tender, drain; cool. Melt extra butter in same pan until lightly browned, stir in pasta, remove from heat. Stir in 1⅓ cups of remaining cheese, stir until well combined.

Spread half the pasta mixture into greased 11 inch x 13 inch baking pan. Top with half the meat sauce, then remaining pasta mixture, spread with remaining meat sauce. Top with cheese sauce, sprinkle with combined bread crumbs, nutmeg and remaining cheese. Bake in 350°F oven about 40 minutes or until top is lightly browned.

Meat Sauce: Heat butter in pan, add onions and garlic, cook, stirring, until onions are soft. Add beef, cook, stirring, until well browned. Stir in tomatoes, paste, sugar, cloves, bay leaf and cinnamon, simmer, uncovered, for 20 minutes. Remove cloves and bay leaf; cool. Stir in lightly beaten egg whites.

Serves 8.

■ Slice best made a day ahead.
■ Storage: Covered, in refrigerator.
■ Freeze: Suitable.
■ Microwave: Pasta suitable.

EASY PASTRAMI AND PIMIENTO STIR-FRY

⅓ cup olive oil
2 onions, sliced
2 cloves garlic, minced
½lb twisted pasta sticks
13oz can pimientos, drained, sliced
¼lb pastrami, sliced
3 tablespoons chopped fresh parsley

Heat oil in pan, add onions and garlic, cook, stirring, until onions are soft.

Add pasta to large pan of boiling water, boil, uncovered, until just tender; drain.

Add pasta, pimientos, pastrami and parsley to onion mixture, stir until heated through.

Serves 4.

■ Recipe best made just before serving.
■ Freeze: Not suitable.
■ Microwave: Pasta suitable.

RIGHT: From left: Cheesy Spaghetti and Beef Slice, Easy Pastrami and Pimiento Stir-Fry.

HERBED MEATBALL BAKE WITH CREAMY BACON SAUCE

1lb rigatoni pasta
⅓ cup grated fresh Parmesan cheese

MEATBALLS
1 slice white bread, chopped
¼ cup milk
1½lb ground beef
1 onion, grated
1 clove garlic, minced
¼ cup grated fresh Parmesan cheese
3 tablespoons chopped fresh parsley
3 tablespoons chopped fresh basil
oil for shallow-frying

SAUCE
5oz slices bacon, chopped
½ cup (1 stick) butter
½ cup all-purpose flour
5 cups milk
¼ cup dry white wine
2 tablespoons seeded mustard
3 tablespoons chopped fresh chives

Add pasta to large pan of boiling water, boil, uncovered, until just tender; drain.

Combine pasta and meatballs in greased ovenproof dish (10 cup capacity). Top with sauce, sprinkle with cheese. Bake, uncovered, in 350°F oven about 15 minutes or until heated through.
Meatballs: Combine bread and milk in bowl; stand 5 minutes. Combine bread mixture, beef, onion, garlic, cheese and herbs in bowl; mix well. Roll 2 rounded tablespoons of mixture into a ball, repeat with remaining mixture.

Shallow-fry meatballs in hot oil until well browned and cooked through; drain on absorbent paper.
Sauce: Add bacon to pan, cook, stirring, until crisp; remove from pan. Melt butter in pan, add flour, stir over heat until bubbling. Remove from heat, stir in milk and wine, stir over heat until sauce boils and thickens. Stir in mustard, chives and bacon.

Serves 6.

■ Recipe can be made a day head.
■ Storage: Covered, in refrigerator.
■ Freeze: Not suitable.
■ Microwave: Pasta and sauce suitable.

TASTY BEEF AND SPAGHETTI CASSEROLE

½lb spinach spaghetti pasta
2 tablespoons olive oil
1 onion, finely chopped
1 clove garlic, minced
1lb ground beef
15oz can tomato puree
¼lb mushrooms, sliced
2 tablespoons chopped fresh parsley
2 teaspoons sugar
½ cup grated fresh Parmesan cheese

SAUCE
2 tablespoons (¼ stick) butter
2 tablespoons all-purpose flour
1⅓ cups milk

Add pasta to large pan of boiling water, boil, uncovered, until just tender; drain.

Heat oil in pan, add onion and garlic, cook, stirring until onion is soft. Add beef, cook, stirring, until browned. Stir in puree, simmer, covered, 15 minutes. Stir in mushrooms, parsley and sugar, simmer, uncovered, further 5 minutes.

Spread half the pasta into greased ovenproof dish (8 cup capacity). Top with beef mixture, then remaining pasta, pour over sauce; sprinkle with cheese. Bake in a 375°F oven about 15 minutes or until lightly browned.
Sauce: Melt butter in pan, add flour, stir over heat until bubbling. Remove from heat, gradually stir in milk, stir over heat until sauce boils and thickens.

Serves 4.

■ Recipe can be made a day ahead.
■ Storage: Covered, in refrigerator.
■ Freeze: Suitable.
■ Microwave: Pasta and sauce suitable.

RUMP STEAK WITH BRANDIED BLUE CHEESE SAUCE

1lb rump steak
1 tablespoon olive oil
1lb spinach fettuccine pasta
1 green onion, thinly sliced

SAUCE
3 tablespoons butter
1 onion, chopped
2 tablespoons all-purpose flour
1 cup water
1 small chicken bouillon cube, crumbled
½ cup milk
7oz blue cheese, crumbled
1 tablespoon brandy
1 clove garlic, minced

Cut steak into 2 inch pieces. Heat oil in pan, add steak, cook over high heat until well browned and done as desired. Remove from heat; keep warm.

Just before serving, cut steak into thin strips. Add pasta to large pan of boiling water, boil, uncovered, until just tender; drain. Combine pasta, sauce and steak, top with onion.
Sauce: Melt butter in pan, add onion, cook, stirring, until soft. Add flour, stir until bubbling. Remove from heat, gradually stir in combined water, bouillon cube and milk. Stir over heat until mixture boils and thickens, simmer, uncovered, for 3 minutes; cool slightly.

Blend or process sauce, cheese, brandy and garlic until smooth.

Serves 6.

■ Recipe best made just before serving.
■ Freeze: Not suitable.
■ Microwave: Pasta suitable.

LEFT: Clockwise from back: Rump Steak with Brandied Blue Cheese Sauce, Tasty Beef and Spaghetti Casserole, Herbed Meatball Bake with Creamy Bacon Sauce.

CILANTRO MEATBALLS
WITH GINGER PLUM SAUCE

2 tablespoons oil
1 onion, chopped
1 clove garlic, minced
1lb ground beef
1 cup (2½oz) fresh bread crumbs
1 egg, lightly beaten
2 teaspoons chopped fresh cilantro
oil for deep-frying
7oz fresh egg noodles

SAUCE
6 Chinese dried mushrooms
2in piece fresh gingerroot
1 tablespoon olive oil
1 onion, thinly sliced
1 clove garlic, minced
¼ cup dry sherry
2½ cups water
**1 small chicken bouillon cube,
    crumbled**
¼ cup plum sauce
¼lb snow peas
2 green onions, chopped
1 tablespoon cornstarch
2 tablespoons water, extra

Heat oil in pan, add onion and garlic, cook, stirring, until onion is soft. Combine beef, bread crumbs, egg, cilantro and onion mixture in bowl; mix well. Shape rounded

tablespoons of mixture into balls using floured hands, place on tray; cover, refrigerate 1 hour.

Deep-fry meatballs in hot oil until well browned and cooked through; drain on absorbent paper. Add meatballs to sauce, keep warm.

Add noodles to large pan of boiling water, boil, uncovered, until just tender; drain; serve with meatballs and sauce.
Sauce: Place mushrooms in bowl, cover with boiling water, stand 20 minutes. Drain mushrooms. Discard stems, slice caps thinly. Cut gingerroot into thin strips.

Heat oil in pan, add onion, garlic and gingerroot, cook, stirring, until onion is soft. Add sherry, bring to boil, simmer, un-covered, 1 minute. Stir in combined water, bouillon cube and sauce, bring to boil, simmer, uncovered, for 15 minutes. Add mushrooms, peas and green onions to pan, simmer 1 minute. Stir in blended cornstarch and extra water, stir over heat until sauce boils and thickens.

Serves 4.

■ Meatballs and sauce can be made a
  day ahead.
■ Storage: Covered, in refrigerator.
■ Freeze: Cooked meatballs suitable.
■ Microwave: Noodles suitable.

HOT PASTRAMI
AND ARTICHOKE SALAD

1¼lb sliced pastrami
¼ cup olive oil
**2 x 14oz cans artichoke hearts,
    drained, quartered**
⅓ cup sugar
1¼ cups dry red wine
1 red bell pepper, sliced
½ cup black olives
¼ cup shredded fresh basil leaves
10oz rigatoni pasta
15 small fresh basil leaves, extra

Cut pastrami into thin strips. Heat oil in pan, add artichokes, cook, stirring, until lightly browned. Add pastrami, sugar and wine, bring to boil, simmer, uncovered, for 3 minutes. Add pepper, olives and shredded basil; cook 2 minutes.

Add pasta to large pan of boiling water, boil, uncovered, until just tender; drain.

Combine pasta with pastrami mixture and extra basil leaves.

Serves 4.

■ Recipe best made close to serving.
■ Freeze: Not suitable.
■ Microwave: Pasta suitable.

QUICK AND EASY LASAGNE

2 tablespoons olive oil
1 onion, finely chopped
1 clove garlic, minced
1lb ground beef
2 x 16oz jars pasta sauce
8oz (16) instant lasagne pasta sheets
1lb ricotta cheese
½ cup milk
½lb mozzarella cheese, shredded
½ cup heavy cream
¼ cup grated fresh Parmesan cheese

Heat oil in pan, add onion and garlic, cook, stirring, until onion is soft. Add beef, cook, stirring, until well browned. Stir in pasta sauce, cook until heated through; remove from heat.

Line shallow greased 8 inch x 12 inch ovenproof dish with a layer of pasta, top with one-third of beef mixture. Spread with one-third of combined ricotta cheese and milk, sprinkle with one-third of mozzarella cheese. Repeat layering, finishing with pasta; pour over cream, sprinkle with Parmesan cheese.

Bake in 350°F oven about 40 minutes or until pasta is tender. Cover lasagne with foil during cooking if surface begins to brown too quickly.

Serves 6.

■ Recipe can be made 2 days ahead.
■ Storage: Covered, in refrigerator.
■ Freeze: Not suitable.
■ Microwave: Not suitable.

LEFT: Cilantro Meatballs with Ginger Plum Sauce.
BELOW: From back: Quick and Easy Lasagne, Hot Pastrami and Artichoke Salad.

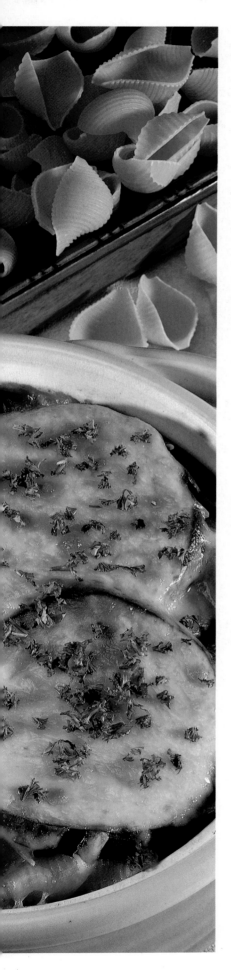

CHEESE-TOPPED BEEF AND EGGPLANT BAKE

2 (about 1½lb) eggplants
salt
3 cups (7oz) shell pasta
¼ cup olive oil
1 onion, chopped
2 cloves garlic, minced
3 tomatoes, chopped
⅓ cup tomato paste
1½ cups water
2 teaspoons sugar
3 (about 10oz) zucchini, chopped
1 large red bell pepper, chopped
1lb piece beef tenderloin, sliced
1 teaspoon dried tarragon leaves
2 cups (7oz) shredded
    mozzarella cheese
3 tablespoons chopped fresh parsley

Cut eggplants into ½ inch slices, place on wire rack, sprinkle with salt, stand 30 minutes. Rinse eggplant under cold water, drain on absorbent paper.

Add pasta to large pan of boiling water, boil, uncovered, until just tender; drain.

Heat oil in pan, add onion and garlic, cook, stirring, until onion is soft. Stir in tomatoes, paste, water and sugar, simmer, uncovered, for 10 minutes. Stir in zucchini, pepper, beef and tarragon, simmer further 15 minutes. Stir in pasta, simmer, uncovered, until mixture is slightly thickened.

Spread one-third of beef mixture into greased ovenproof dish (10 cup capacity), top with a layer of eggplant. Repeat layering, finishing with eggplant.

Just before serving, sprinkle with cheese, bake in 350°F oven about 25 minutes or until eggplant is tender and cheese is lightly browned. Serve sprinkled with parsley.

Serves 6.

■ Recipe can be prepared a day ahead.
■ Storage: Covered, in refrigerator.
■ Freeze: Not suitable.
■ Microwave: Pasta suitable.

DOUBLE-FRIED SHREDDED BEEF WITH TAGLIATELLE

1½lb piece rump steak
⅓ cup cornstarch
2 tablespoons dark soy sauce
1 tablespoon oil
1 teaspoon five-spice powder
½ teaspoon chili powder
½ teaspoon ground gingerroot
2 carrots
oil for deep-frying
½lb tagliatelle pasta
2 green onions, sliced
2 tablespoons (¼ stick) butter

Remove excess fat from steak; wrap steak in plastic wrap, freeze about 30 minutes or until partially frozen. Slice steak thinly, cut slices into fine shreds. Combine steak, cornstarch, sauce, oil and spices in bowl; cover, refrigerate 1 hour.

Thinly slice carrots lengthways, cut into fine strips.

Deep-fry steak mixture in hot oil in several batches until lightly browned and crisp, stirring to separate steak; drain on absorbent paper.

Just before serving, add pasta to large pan of boiling water, boil, uncovered, until just tender; drain. Return pasta to pan, stir in onions and butter; keep warm.

Reheat oil, deep-fry steak and carrots until steak is well browned; drain on absorbent paper. Serve steak and carrots over pasta mixture.

Serves 4.

■ Steak can be prepared a day ahead. Deep-frying can begin 1 hour ahead.
■ Storage: Covered, in refrigerator.
■ Freeze: Not suitable.
■ Microwave: Pasta suitable.

LEFT: From left: Double-Fried Shredded Beef with Tagliatelle, Cheese-Topped Beef and Eggplant Bake.

STIR-FRIED CHILI GARLIC STEAK WITH POTATOES

1 onion, chopped
4 cloves garlic, minced
1½ teaspoons dried chili flakes
1 tablespoon sugar
½ teaspoon dried shrimp paste
4 baby potatoes
2 tomatoes, peeled
3 tablespoons oil
1lb rump steak, thinly sliced
6 green onions, chopped
3 cups (½lb) shredded
   Chinese cabbage
¼lb bean sprouts
¾lb fresh egg noodles
3 tablespoons light soy sauce
2 tablespoons sweet chili sauce

Blend or process onion, garlic, chili flakes, sugar and paste until smooth.

Boil, steam or microwave potatoes until just tender; cut into quarters. Cut tomatoes into wedges.

Heat half the oil in wok or pan, add onion mixture, stir-fry for 2 minutes. Add steak to wok in batches, stir-fry until well browned and tender; remove from pan.

Heat remaining oil in wok, add onions, cabbage, sprouts and tomatoes, stir-fry until cabbage is wilted. Return steak to wok with noodles, stir in sauces, stir-fry until heated through. Serve with potatoes.

Serves 4.

■ Recipe best made close to serving.
■ Freeze: Not suitable.
■ Microwave: Potatoes suitable.

BEST EVER BOLOGNAISE SAUCE

2 tablespoons olive oil
2 onions, chopped
1 clove garlic, minced
2lb ground beef
2 x 14½oz cans tomatoes
1½ cups water
½ cup dry white wine
3 tablespoons tomato paste
3 small beef bouillon cubes, crumbled
1 teaspoon dried oregano leaves
½ teaspoon dried marjoram leaves
½ teaspoon sugar

COOL 'N' SPICY BEEF WITH PASTA

7oz pipe rigate pasta
1 tablespoon olive oil
1lb ground beef
1 teaspoon ground coriander
1 teaspoon ground cumin
½ teaspoon ground cardamom
½ teaspoon garam masala
1 large red bell pepper
5oz snow peas, chopped
5 green onions, chopped
2 teaspoons chopped fresh cilantro
¾ cup pitted dates, sliced

DRESSING
2 tablespoons light soy sauce
¼ cup dry sherry
1 tablespoon mirin
2 teaspoons sugar
2 teaspoons Oriental sesame oil
2 teaspoons grated fresh gingerroot

Add pasta to large pan of boiling water, boil, uncovered, until just tender; drain.

Heat oil in pan, add beef and ground spices, cook, stirring, until well browned and tender; cool.

Quarter pepper, remove seeds and membrane. Broil pepper, skin-side-up, until skin blisters and blackens. Remove skin, chop pepper. Combine beef mixture, pepper, snow peas, onions and pasta in bowl; cover, refrigerate.

Just before serving, stir in fresh cilantro, dates and dressing; mix well.

Dressing: Combine all ingredients in jar; shake well.

Serves 6.

■ Salad can be made a day ahead.
  Dressing can be made 3 days ahead.
■ Storage: Covered, in refrigerator.
■ Freeze: Not suitable.
■ Microwave: Pasta suitable.

LEFT: From left: Stir-Fried Chili Garlic Steak with Potatoes, Cool 'n' Spicy Beef with Pasta.
BELOW: Best Ever Bolognaise Sauce.

Heat oil in pan, add onions and garlic, cook, stirring, over low heat about 15 minutes or until onions are very soft. Add beef, cook, stirring, until well browned. Stir in undrained crushed tomatoes, water, wine, paste, bouillon cubes, herbs and sugar. Bring to boil, simmer, uncovered, about 2 hours or until sauce is thickened; stirring occasionally. Serve with pasta and grated Parmesan cheese, if desired.

Serves 4.

■ Bolognaise sauce can be made
  2 days ahead.
■ Storage: Covered, in refrigerator.
■ Freeze: Suitable.
■ Microwave: Not suitable.

LAMB

It's deliciously easy to serve lamb in tempting new ways when you add plenty of pasta, and these recipes abound in the unusual. For example, there's our cheesy, creamy torte or the clever coil of pasta with a hearty filling. Then there's green pea ravioli with minted lamb salad, honeyed lamb with noodles, and a quick chili garlic lamb and noodle stir-fry. Favorites with a difference include lasagne, cannelloni, and, of course, roast lamb, only this time with pasta and a thick tomato sauce.

HONEYED LAMB WITH NOODLES AND OMELET

¾lb fresh egg noodles
1½lb lamb fillets
cornstarch
oil for deep-frying
½ teaspoon ground gingerroot
¼ cup honey
½ cup lemon juice
½ cup water
2 teaspoons cornstarch, extra
1 tablespoon light soy sauce
2 green onions, sliced

OMELET
1 tablespoon milk
1 egg
1 teaspoon oil

Add noodles to large pan of boiling water, boil, uncovered, about 5 minutes or until just tender, drain; keep warm.

Cut each lamb fillet into 1½ inch pieces, pound each piece until thin. Toss lamb in cornstarch, shake away excess cornstarch. Deep-fry lamb in hot oil until well browned and tender; drain on absorbent paper.

Combine gingerroot, honey, juice and water in pan, stir in blended extra cornstarch and sauce. Stir over heat until sauce boils and thickens. Add lamb, stir until heated through, add onions. Serve honeyed lamb over noodles, top with omelet.
Omelet: Beat milk and egg in bowl. Heat oil in large pan, add egg mixture, cook about 3 minutes or until set; cool. Roll omelet tightly, slice finely.

Serves 4.

■ Recipe best made close to serving.
■ Freeze: Not suitable.
■ Microwave: Noodles suitable.

CREAMY LAMB AND CHICKEN PASTA COIL

1lb ziti pasta
5oz mushrooms, chopped
1⅓ cups (7oz) chopped cooked chicken
18 pitted black olives, halved
3 tablespoons chopped fresh basil

WHITE SAUCE
½ cup (1 stick) butter
½ cup all-purpose flour
2 cups milk
¾ cup grated cheddar cheese

LAMB SAUCE
1 tablespoon olive oil
1 onion, finely chopped
2 cloves garlic, minced
1lb ground lamb
14½oz can tomatoes
3 tablespoons tomato paste
3 tablespoons chopped fresh basil

Add pasta to large pan of boiling water, boil, uncovered, for three-quarters the recommended cooking time on packet; drain. Make white sauce and lamb sauce.

Line a lightly greased ovenproof bowl (14 cup capacity) by coiling with half the pasta. Cut half the remaining pasta into 2 inch lengths; reserve uncut pasta.

Spread one-third of the warm white sauce evenly over pasta in bowl, place one-third of lamb sauce into bowl, top with half the chopped pasta.

Spread a little more white sauce over pasta. Top with half each of the mushrooms, chicken, olives and basil, half the remaining lamb sauce, then remaining chopped pasta.

Spread chopped pasta with half the remaining white sauce, top with remaining mushrooms, chicken, olives and basil. Spread with remaining lamb sauce.

Finish by coiling reserved uncut pasta over lamb sauce, spread with remaining white sauce.

Cover bowl with greased paper, then foil, place bowl in roasting pan, pour in enough boiling water to come halfway up side of bowl. Bake in 350°F oven for 45 minutes. Discard paper and foil, cool bowl to room temperature. Turn pasta coil out just before serving.
White Sauce: Melt butter in pan, stir in flour, stir over heat until bubbling. Remove from heat, gradually stir in milk, stir over heat until sauce boils and thickens. Remove from heat, stir in cheese.
Lamb Sauce: Heat oil in pan, add onion and garlic, cook, stirring, until onion is soft. Add lamb, cook, stirring, until well browned. Stir in undrained crushed tomatoes, paste and basil. Simmer, uncovered, about 10 minutes or until thickened.

Serves 6.

■ Recipe can be made 2 days ahead.
■ Storage: Covered, in refrigerator.
■ Freeze: Not suitable.
■ Microwave: Pasta and white sauce suitable.

RIGHT: From back: Creamy Lamb and Chicken Pasta Coil, Honeyed Lamb with Noodles and Omelet.

LAMB, CHEESE AND EGGPLANT TORTE

2 medium (about 1¼lb)
    eggplants, sliced
salt
⅓ cup olive oil
1 tablespoon olive oil, extra
1lb ground lamb
1 teaspoon ground cinnamon
1 teaspoon ground cumin
3 tablespoons tomato paste
14½oz can tomatoes
2 small chicken bouillon cubes,
    crumbled
½ teaspoon sugar
2 cups (7oz) pasta twists
7oz fresh goats' milk cheese,
    crumbled
1½ cups (5oz) shredded mozzarella
    cheese
1 green bell pepper, chopped
2 tablespoons chopped fresh mint

Line base and side of deep 9 inch round baking pan with paper, grease paper. Place eggplant slices on wire rack, sprinkle with salt, stand 20 minutes. Rinse eggplant slices under cold water, drain on absorbent paper.

Heat oil in pan, add eggplant in batches, cook on both sides until well browned; drain on absorbent paper.

Heat extra oil in pan, add lamb, cook, stirring, until well browned. Add spices, paste, undrained crushed tomatoes, bouillon cubes and sugar. Bring to boil, simmer, uncovered, about 10 minutes or until thickened.

Add pasta to large pan of boiling water, boil, uncovered, until just tender; drain.

Combine pasta with lamb mixture in bowl. Combine cheeses, pepper and mint in separate bowl.

Place a layer of eggplant into prepared pan, spread with half the lamb mixture, top with half the cheese mixture. Repeat layering, finishing with an eggplant layer; press firmly into pan. Cover pan with foil, place pan in roasting pan, pour in enough boiling water to come halfway up side of baking pan. Bake in 350°F oven 1 hour. Stand pan 10 minutes before turning out. Serve torte hot or cold, sprinkled with extra goats' milk cheese, if desired.

Serves 8.
■ Recipe can be made a day ahead.
■ Storage: Covered, in refrigerator.
■ Freeze: Not suitable.
■ Microwave: Pasta suitable.

CHILI GARLIC LAMB AND NOODLE STIR-FRY

1lb lamb fillets, sliced
3 tablespoons chili sauce
3 tablespoons hoisin sauce
3 tablespoons sweet sherry
2 cloves garlic, sliced
1lb fresh egg noodles
3 tablespoons vegetable oil
2 tablespoons vegetable oil, extra
1 bunch Chinese broccoli, chopped
1 teaspoon cornstarch
½ cup water
2 tablespoons light soy sauce
2 teaspoons peanut butter

Combine lamb, chili sauce, hoisin sauce, sherry and garlic in bowl; cover, refrigerate 1 hour. Place noodles in bowl, cover with boiling water, stand 5 minutes; drain.

Heat half the oil in wok or pan, add half the lamb mixture, stir-fry until browned all over, remove from wok. Repeat with remaining oil and lamb.

Heat extra oil in wok, add broccoli, stir-fry until lightly cooked. Stir in blended cornstarch and water, soy sauce and peanut butter, stir until mixture boils and thickens. Add lamb and noodles, stir until heated through.

Serves 6.
■ Lamb can be prepared a day ahead.
■ Storage: Covered, in refrigerator.
■ Freeze: Not suitable.
■ Microwave: Not suitable.

ROAST LAMB WITH TOMATO ROSEMARY SAUCE

4lb leg of lamb
3 cloves garlic, sliced
6 small sprigs fresh rosemary
2 tablespoons olive oil
2 onions, sliced
2 x 14½oz cans tomatoes
2 tablespoons cornstarch
2 tablespoons water
1lb tagliatelle pasta
1 cup (2½oz) grated fresh
    Parmesan cheese

Score lamb at ¾ inch intervals using sharp knife. Push garlic and rosemary into scores, brush lamb with oil. Place lamb in roasting pan, bake in 400°F oven 15 minutes, add onions and undrained crushed tomatoes to dish. Cover dish with foil, bake in 350°F oven about 1 hour or until done as desired. Remove lamb from sauce, cover, keep warm.

Combine sauce with blended cornstarch and water in pan, stir over heat until sauce boils and thickens.

Add pasta to large pan of boiling water, boil, uncovered, until just tender; drain. Combine pasta with sauce, serve with sliced lamb; sprinkle with cheese.

Serves 8.
■ Recipe best made just before serving.
■ Freeze: Not suitable.
■ Microwave: Pasta suitable.

RIGHT: Lamb, Cheese and Eggplant Torte.
FAR RIGHT: From back: Chili Garlic Lamb and Noodle Stir-Fry, Roast Lamb with Tomato Rosemary Sauce.

CREAMY ASPARAGUS FETTUCCINE WITH LAMB

1 tablespoon olive oil
1lb lamb fillets, sliced
2 bunches (about 1lb) fresh
    asparagus
3 tablespoons butter
2 green onions, chopped
1 small sprig fresh rosemary
1¼ cups heavy cream
½ cup grated fresh Parmesan cheese
¾lb fettuccine pasta

Heat oil in pan, add lamb, cook over high heat until browned all over. Remove from pan, drain on absorbent paper; keep warm.

    Cut tips from asparagus, reserve tips. Cut stalks into ¾ inch lengths. Melt butter in pan, add stalks and onions, cook, stirring, until asparagus is tender. Add rosemary and cream to pan, bring to boil, simmer, uncovered, 10 minutes. Remove from heat, discard rosemary. Blend or process asparagus mixture until smooth, stir in cheese. Boil, steam or microwave reserved asparagus tips until tender; drain.

    Add pasta to large pan of boiling water, boil, uncovered, until just tender; drain.

    Combine pasta, lamb, asparagus sauce and asparagus tips in pan, cook until heated through.

Serves 6.

■ Recipe best made just before serving.
■ Freeze: Not suitable.
■ Microwave: Pasta and asparagus suitable.

LAMB RAVIOLI WITH MINTED YOGURT

2 tablespoons olive oil
1 small onion, finely chopped
1 clove garlic, minced
7oz ground lamb
1 teaspoon curry powder
1 teaspoon ground cumin
1 teaspoon cornstarch
¼ cup water
2 quantities plain pasta dough

MINTED YOGURT
2 cups plain yogurt
2 tablespoons chopped fresh mint
2 tablespoons chopped fresh basil

Heat oil in pan, add onion and garlic, cook, stirring, until onion is soft. Add lamb, curry powder and cumin, cook, stirring, until lamb is browned. Stir in blended cornstarch and water, bring to boil; cool.

Roll pasta dough until ⅛ inch thick, cut into 1¾ inch rounds, top half the rounds with ½ level teaspoon of lamb mixture. Brush edges of rounds with water, top with remaining rounds, press edges together. **Just before serving,** add ravioli to large pan of boiling water, boil, uncovered, for about 8 minutes or until just tender; drain. Combine ravioli with minted yogurt.
Minted Yogurt: Combine all ingredients in bowl; mix well.

Serves 4.

- ■ Pasta and sauce can be prepared a day ahead.
- ■ Storage: Covered, in refrigerator.
- ■ Freeze: Cooked pasta suitable.
- ■ Microwave: Not suitable.

LAMB CANNELLONI WITH CREAMY HERB SAUCE

¼lb instant cannelloni pasta

FILLING
2 tablespoons olive oil
¾lb ground lamb
14½oz can tomatoes
2 tablespoons tomato paste
2 tablespoons dry red wine
2 tablespoons chopped fresh chives
¼ cup grated fresh Parmesan cheese
¼ teaspoon sugar

CREAMY HERB SAUCE
1¼ cups heavy cream
¼ cup chopped fresh chives
¼ cup chopped fresh parsley
1 tablespoon chopped fresh marjoram
½ cup milk
½ teaspoon seeded mustard
1 tablespoon cornstarch
2 tablespoons dry white wine

Fill pasta with filling, place in single layer in greased shallow ovenproof dish. Pour sauce over cannelloni, bake, covered, in 350°F oven about 30 minutes or until pasta is tender.
Filling: Heat oil in pan, add lamb, cook, stirring, until well browned. Stir in undrained crushed tomatoes, paste and wine. Bring to boil, simmer, uncovered, about 5 minutes or until thickened. Stir in chives, cheese and sugar; cool.
Creamy Herb Sauce: Heat cream in pan, add herbs, milk and mustard, bring to boil. Stir in blended cornstarch and wine, stir until sauce boils and thickens.

Serves 4.

- ■ Recipe can be made a day ahead.
- ■ Storage: Covered, in refrigerator.
- ■ Freeze: Suitable.
- ■ Microwave: Suitable.

ABOVE LEFT: Clockwise from back: Creamy Asparagus Fettuccine with Lamb, Lamb Ravioli with Minted Yogurt, Lamb Cannelloni with Creamy Herb Sauce.

FRUITY LAMB NOISETTES WITH ORANGE SAUCE

1 tablespoon orzo pasta
2 green onions, finely chopped
1½oz sliced cooked ham, chopped
2oz ricotta cheese
½ teaspoon grated orange zest
¼ teaspoon chopped dried rosemary
1 tablespoon finely chopped dried papaya
1½lb boned loin of lamb
⅓ quantity herbed pasta dough
all-purpose flour
2 tablespoons (¼ stick) butter, melted

ORANGE SAUCE
3 tablespoons dry white wine
3 tablespoons white wine vinegar
1 teaspoon grated orange zest
1 cup (2 sticks) butter, chopped
2 green onions, chopped

Add orzo to pan of boiling water, boil, uncovered, until just tender, drain; cool.

Combine orzo, onions, ham, cheese, zest, rosemary and papaya in bowl. Spread mixture over inside of lamb, roll up, secure with kitchen string. Bake in 450°F oven 20 minutes, reduce heat to 350°F, bake further 40 minutes or until cooked as desired.

Roll herbed pasta until ⅛ inch thick, cut into ¾ inch strips; sprinkle with flour.
Just before serving, cut lamb into ¾ inch pieces. Add herbed pasta to large pan of boiling water, boil, uncovered, until just tender; drain. Wrap a strip of pasta around each piece of lamb, secure with toothpicks, place on baking sheet, brush pasta with butter. Bake noisettes in 375°F oven about 20 minutes or until pasta is crisp. Serve with orange sauce.
Orange Sauce: Combine wine, vinegar and zest in pan, bring to boil, simmer, uncovered, until reduced to 4 teaspoons. Gradually whisk in cold butter. Add the onions, mix lightly.

Serves 4.

- ■ Lamb can be cooked a day ahead. Sauce best made just before serving.
- ■ Storage: Covered, in refrigerator.
- ■ Freeze: Lamb suitable.
- ■ Microwave: Pasta suitable.

BELOW: Fruity Lamb Noisettes with Orange Sauce.

WHOLE-WHEAT PASTA AND LAMB LASAGNE

½ quantity whole-wheat pasta dough
1 tablespoon olive oil
1 onion, sliced
2 cloves garlic, minced
4 (about ¾lb) zucchini, sliced
2 teaspoons grated lemon zest
1 tablespoon olive oil, extra
2 cloves garlic, minced, extra
1½lb ground lamb
1 small beef bouillon cube, crumbled
¼ cup chopped fresh parsley
¼ cup chopped fresh basil
3 tablespoons lemon juice
10oz jarlsberg cheese, sliced
3½oz jarlsberg cheese, grated, extra
½ cup heavy cream

Lightly grease shallow 7 inch x 10 inch ovenproof dish. Roll pasta dough until ⅛ inch thick, trim sheets to fit prepared dish. Add pasta to large pan of boiling water, boil, uncovered, until just tender; drain.

Heat oil in pan, add onion and garlic, cook, stirring, until onion is soft. Add zucchini and zest, cook, stirring, until zucchini is lightly browned; remove from pan.

Heat extra oil in pan, add extra garlic and lamb, cook, stirring, until lamb is well browned and any liquid has evaporated. Add bouillon cube, herbs and juice, cook 1 minute.

Place 1 layer of pasta into prepared dish, spread with one-third each of the lamb mixture, zucchini mixture and sliced cheese. Repeat layering, finishing with pasta layer. Top with grated extra cheese, pour cream evenly over surface. Bake, uncovered, in 350°F oven about 30 minutes or until lightly browned and lasagne is heated through.

Serves 6.

■ Recipe can be made a day ahead.
■ Storage: Covered, in refrigerator.
■ Freeze: Suitable.
■ Microwave: Pasta suitable.

ABOVE: Clockwise from front: Lamb with Broccoli in Red Wine Sauce, Whole-Wheat Pasta and Lamb Lasagne, Meatballs in Herbed Tomato Sauce.
RIGHT: Minted Green Pea Ravioli and Lamb Salad.

LAMB WITH BROCCOLI IN RED WINE SAUCE

¼ cup olive oil
1 onion, chopped
1 carrot, chopped
1 clove garlic, minced
½ cup sweet sherry
1 cup dry red wine
5 cups water
2 large beef bouillon cubes, crumbled
1 bay leaf
1 tablespoon sugar
1lb broccoli, chopped
1 red bell pepper, chopped
¼ cup cornstarch
¼ cup water, extra
1 tablespoon heavy cream
10oz spaghetti pasta
¼ cup olive oil, extra
1¼lb lamb fillets, thinly sliced

Heat oil in pan, add onion and carrot, cook, stirring, until well browned. Add garlic, sherry, wine, water, bouillon cubes, bay leaf and sugar. Bring to boil, simmer, covered, 20 minutes. Strain mixture, discard vegetables.

Return liquid to pan, bring to boil, boil, uncovered, about 10 minutes, or until reduced by one-third. Add broccoli and pepper, boil until vegetables are tender. Stir in blended cornstarch and extra water, stir until sauce boils and thickens, stir in cream; keep warm.

Add pasta to large pan of boiling water, boil, uncovered, until just tender, drain.

Heat extra oil in pan, add lamb, cook until well browned and tender. Combine lamb with sauce, serve with warm pasta.

Serves 4.

■ Sauce can be made a day ahead.
■ Storage: Covered, in refrigerator.
■ Freeze: Not suitable.
■ Microwave: Pasta suitable.

MINTED GREEN PEA RAVIOLI AND LAMB SALAD

1¼lb lamb fillets
1 teaspoon cracked black
    peppercorns
1 clove garlic, minced
1 tablespoon olive oil
1 quantity plain pasta dough

GREEN PEA FILLING
1½ cups (6oz) fresh or frozen peas
3 tablespoons butter
1 onion, chopped
2 tablespoons chopped fresh mint

MINT DRESSING
¼ cup olive oil
2 tablespoons cider vinegar
½ teaspoon sugar
2 tablespoons shredded fresh
    mint leaves

Combine lamb, pepper and garlic in bowl; cover, refrigerate 1 hour. Heat oil in pan, add lamb mixture, cook about 5 minutes until well browned all over and tender,

drain on absorbent paper; cool.

Cut lamb into thin slices. Roll pasta dough until ⅛ inch thick, cut into 1¾ inch rounds. Top half the rounds with ½ level teaspoons of pea filling, brush edges of rounds with water, top with remaining rounds, press edges to seal.

Add ravioli to large pan of boiling water, boil, uncovered, about 5 minutes or until just tender; drain. Rinse ravioli under cold water, drain; cool. Combine ravioli, lamb and mint dressing in bowl.

Green Pea Filling: Boil, steam or microwave peas until soft, drain. Heat butter in pan, add onion, cook, stirring, until soft. Blend or process peas, onion mixture and mint until combined, but not smooth.

Mint Dressing: Combine all ingredients in jar; shake well.

Serves 6.

■ Ravioli can be prepared a day ahead. Salad can be made 2 hours ahead.
■ Storage: Covered, in refrigerator.
■ Freeze: Uncooked ravioli suitable.
■ Microwave: Filling suitable.

MEATBALLS IN HERBED TOMATO SAUCE

1½lb ground lamb
1 onion, chopped
2 cloves garlic, minced
1 small beef bouillon cube, crumbled
1½ cups (3½oz) fresh bread crumbs
1 egg, lightly beaten
all-purpose flour
3 tablespoons olive oil
1lb spaghetti pasta
3 tablespoons grated
    Parmesan cheese

ball, repeat with remaining mixture; cover, refrigerate 30 minutes.

Toss meatballs in flour, shake away excess flour. Heat oil in pan, add meatballs, cook until well browned all over; drain on absorbent paper.

Add pasta to large pan of boiling water, boil, uncovered, until just tender, drain; keep warm.

Just before serving, add meatballs to sauce, cover, simmer about 10 minutes or until meatballs are cooked. Sprinkle meatball sauce with Parmesan cheese; serve with spaghetti.

Sauce: Heat oil in pan, add onion and garlic, cook, stirring, until onion is soft. Stir in undrained crushed tomatoes, paste, herbs, bouillon cube, water and sugar; bring to boil before adding meatballs.

Serves 6.

■ Meatballs can be made a day ahead.
■ Storage: Covered, in refrigerator.
■ Freeze: Meatballs suitable.
■ Microwave: Pasta suitable.

PORK & VEAL

Here you can enjoy tasty pork flavors such as salami, prosciutto, pancetta and cabanossi as well as familiar cuts of both pork and veal. There's a truly luscious pizza with a pasta base, a yummy pork and spinach roll, and little meatballs wrapped around melting, hot mozzarella – all quite hearty, as are the baked frittata and veal lasagne rolls. To tempt you even more, think of pretty salads and great-tasting sauces to make meals (or appetizers) without fuss.

PORK AND MACARONI SALAD

1⅓ cups (7oz) macaroni pasta
½ cup peanut butter
½ cup water
2 teaspoons Oriental sesame oil
2 tablespoons light soy sauce
1 tablespoon lime juice
pinch cayenne pepper
2 small green cucumbers, seeded
5 green onions, chopped
10oz barbequed red pork, sliced
lettuce leaves

Add pasta to large pan of boiling water, boil, uncovered, until just tender; drain. Rinse pasta under cold water; drain.

Combine peanut butter, water, oil, sauce, juice and cayenne in pan, stir over heat until smooth and combined.

Cut cucumbers into strips, combine in bowl with onions, pork and pasta. Pour over peanut butter mixture; mix well. Serve over lettuce leaves.

Serves 4.

■ Recipe can be made 6 hours ahead.
■ Storage: Covered, in refrigerator.
■ Freeze: Not suitable.
■ Microwave: Suitable.

Good:

HERBED PROSCIUTTO, PEPPER AND PASTA BAKE

3 tablespoons olive oil
2 onions, chopped
1 leek, sliced
1 clove garlic, minced
2 small fresh red chili peppers, chopped
1 large red bell pepper, chopped
1 large green bell pepper, chopped
⅓ cup chopped fresh basil
1 teaspoon dried oregano leaves
2 x 14½oz cans tomatoes
½ cup dry white wine
3 tablespoons tomato paste
2 small chicken bouillon cubes, crumbled
1 teaspoon sugar
¼ quantity spinach pasta dough
5oz sliced prosciutto

Heat oil in pan, add onions, leek, garlic and chilies, cook, stirring, until onions and leek are soft. Add peppers, herbs, undrained crushed tomatoes, wine, paste, bouillon cubes and sugar. Bring to boil, simmer, uncovered, 20 minutes.

Cut pasta dough in half, roll each half until ⅛ inch thick. Cut pasta to fit shallow ovenproof dish (6 cup capacity).

Add pasta to large pan of boiling water, boil, uncovered, about 5 minutes or until just tender; drain. Spoon one-third of tomato mixture into dish, top with half the pasta. Place half the prosciutto over pasta. Repeat layering, ending with tomato mixture. Bake, covered, in 350°F oven about 40 minutes or until bake is heated through.

Serves 4.

■ Recipe can be made a day ahead.
■ Storage: Covered, in refrigerator.
■ Freeze: Not suitable.
■ Microwave: Pasta suitable.

BUCATINI WITH PANCETTA AND TOMATOES

½lb bucatini pasta
3 tablespoons olive oil
2 onions, finely chopped
½lb pancetta, chopped
2 x 14½oz cans tomatoes, drained, chopped
4 (5oz) bocconcini cheese, chopped

Add pasta to large pan of boiling water, boil, uncovered, until just tender; drain.

Heat oil in pan, add onions and pancetta, cook, stirring, until onions are soft. Stir in tomatoes, stir over heat 2 minutes. Stir in bocconcini and pasta, stir until heated through.

Serves 4.

■ Recipe best made just before serving.
■ Freeze: Not suitable.
■ Microwave: Pasta suitable.

RIGHT: Clockwise from front: Bucatini with Pancetta and Tomatoes, Pork and Macaroni Salad, Herbed Prosciutto, Pepper and Pasta Bake.

VEAL AND PASTA WITH MUSTARD CREAM SAUCE

¼ cup olive oil
1 onion, sliced
1½lb veal shank
all-purpose flour
½ cup buttermilk
¾ cup heavy cream
½ cup dry white wine
3 tablespoons French mustard
1lb paglia e fieno pasta

Heat 2 tablespoons of the oil in pan, add onion, cook, stirring, until soft; remove from pan.

Remove meat from shank, cut meat into strips. Toss meat in flour, shake away excess flour. Heat remaining oil in pan, add meat, cook, stirring, until well browned and tender; remove from pan, combine with onion in bowl.

Boil any juices remaining in pan on high heat about 1 minute or until reduced to about 4 teaspoons. Add buttermilk to pan, stir over heat until mixture thickens slightly. Stir in cream, wine and mustard, stir until mixture boils, simmer, uncovered, until slightly thickened.

Add pasta to large pan of boiling water, boil, uncovered, until just tender, drain; keep warm.

Add veal and onion to mustard sauce, stir until heated through, serve over pasta.

Serves 4.

■ Recipe best made close to serving.
■ Freeze: Not suitable.
■ Microwave: Pasta suitable.

QUICK TOMATO SAUCE WITH SALAMI AND BASIL

1 tablespoon olive oil
1 onion, thinly sliced
¼lb thinly sliced salami
14½oz can tomatoes
10oz can Tomato Supreme
3 tablespoons chopped fresh basil
2 teaspoons sugar
½lb penne pasta

Heat oil in pan, add onion and salami, cook, stirring, until onion is soft. Stir in undrained crushed tomatoes, Tomato Supreme, basil and sugar. Simmer, uncovered, about 5 minutes or until sauce reduces and thickens.

Add pasta to large pan of boiling water, boil, uncovered, until just tender; drain. Combine pasta with sauce.

Serves 4.

■ Recipe best made just before serving.
■ Freeze: Not suitable.
■ Microwave: Pasta suitable.

CHEESY PORK AND SPINACH ROLL

½ quantity plain pasta dough
¼ cup grated fresh Parmesan cheese
1 tablespoon chopped fresh sage
¼ cup (½ stick) butter, melted

FILLING
½ bunch (10oz) spinach, shredded
2 tablespoons olive oil
1 small onion, finely chopped
1 clove garlic, minced
7oz ground pork and veal
5oz cottage cheese
3½oz neufchatel cheese
1 egg, lightly beaten
½ teaspoon ground nutmeg

Cut pasta dough in half, roll each half to a ⅛ inch thick square. Spread filling over each square, leaving 1¾ inch border. Roll squares tightly as for a jelly-roll.

Wrap rolls in muslin, tie ends, place rolls in large pan filled with boiling salted water.

Boil, uncovered, about 20 minutes, turning rolls occasionally, or until rolls are firm to touch. Remove rolls from water; drain, remove muslin.

Cut rolls into ½ inch slices, arrange in single layer in greased flameproof dish, sprinkle with combined cheese and sage, drizzle with butter. Broil until pasta is lightly browned on the edges.

Filling: Boil, steam or microwave spinach until tender; drain, cool.

Heat oil in pan, add onion and garlic, cook, stirring, until onion is soft. Add pork and veal, cook, stirring, until well browned; cool slightly. Combine cheeses in bowl, stir in egg, nutmeg, pork and veal mixture and spinach; mix well.

Serves 4.

■ Rolls can be made a day ahead.
■ Storage: Covered, in refrigerator.
■ Freeze: Not suitable.
■ Microwave: Spinach suitable.

LEFT: From back: Veal and Pasta with Mustard Cream Sauce, Quick Tomato Sauce with Salami and Basil.
RIGHT: Cheesy Pork and Spinach Roll.

DEEP-FRIED TORTELLINI WITH AVOCADO SAUCE

1lb pork and veal tortellini
all-purpose flour
2 eggs, lightly beaten
packaged unseasoned bread crumbs
oil for deep-frying

AVOCADO SAUCE
1 avocado, chopped
¼ cup milk
1¼ cups heavy cream
1 tablespoon lemon juice
few drops tabasco sauce
2 tablespoons chopped fresh chives

Add tortellini to large pan of boiling water, boil, uncovered, until just tender; drain well on absorbent paper. Toss tortellini in flour, shake away excess flour. Dip tortellini in eggs, then bread crumbs to coat; cover, refrigerate 1 hour.

Just before serving, deep-fry tortellini in hot oil until lightly browned; drain on absorbent paper. Serve hot tortellini with avocado sauce.

Avocado Sauce: Blend or process avocado and milk until smooth. Stir in cream, juice, tabasco and chives.

Serves 4.

■ Tortellini can be made a day ahead.
■ Storage: Covered, in refrigerator.
■ Freeze: Suitable.
■ Microwave: Not suitable.

SPICY PORK STIR-FRY WITH COCONUT MANGO SAUCE

1½lb pork fillets
¼ cup oil
1 onion, chopped
1 teaspoon tandoori curry paste
1 small fresh red chili pepper, chopped
⅔ cup canned unsweetened coconut milk
14oz can mango slices, drained
2 teaspoons lime juice
⅔ cup water
1½ teaspoons paprika
3 zucchini, chopped
1 red bell pepper, chopped
5oz snow peas
10oz thin spaghetti pasta

Cut pork into 2 inch strips. Heat oil in pan, add onion, cook, stirring, until soft. Add pork, curry paste and chili, cook, stirring, until pork is well browned. Stir in coconut milk, mango, juice, water, paprika, zucchini and pepper. Simmer, covered, 3 minutes; then simmer, uncovered, until sauce is slightly thickened. Add peas, simmer 1 minute.

Add pasta to large pan of boiling water, boil, uncovered, until just tender; drain. Serve pasta with pork and sauce.

Serves 6.

■ Recipe best made close to serving.
■ Freeze: Not suitable.
■ Microwave: Pasta suitable.

CHEESY LASAGNE PIZZA

½lb lasagne pasta sheets
1 cup (¼lb) grated cheddar cheese
½lb mushrooms, sliced
1 small green bell pepper, chopped
2 x ¼lb cabanossi sticks, sliced
1½ cups (6oz) grated cheddar cheese, extra
¼ cup grated fresh Parmesan cheese

TOMATO SAUCE
1 tablespoon olive oil
1 onion, chopped
2 cloves garlic, minced
14½oz can tomatoes
3 tablespoons tomato paste
2 tablespoons Worcestershire sauce
3 tablespoons dark brown sugar
1 teaspoon dried basil leaves

Grease 10 inch x 12 inch jelly-roll pan. Add pasta to large pan of boiling water, boil, uncovered, until just tender; drain. Rinse pasta under cold water, drain.

Place half the pasta over base of prepared pan, sprinkle with cheddar cheese, top with remaining pasta. Bake in 350°F oven 10 minutes.

Spread pasta base with tomato sauce, top with mushrooms, pepper and cabanossi. Sprinkle with extra cheddar cheese and Parmesan. Bake in 375°F oven about 40 minutes or until pizza is well browned.

Tomato Sauce: Heat oil in pan, add onion and garlic, cook, stirring, until onion is soft. Add undrained crushed tomatoes, paste, sauce, sugar and basil. Bring to boil, simmer, uncovered, about 20 minutes or until sauce is thickened, stirring occasionally.

Serves 4.

■ Recipe can be made 2 days ahead.
■ Storage: Covered, in refrigerator.
■ Freeze: Cooked or uncooked pizza suitable.
■ Microwave: Pasta suitable.

RIGHT: Clockwise from left: Spicy Pork Stir-Fry with Coconut Mango Sauce, Deep-Fried Tortellini with Avocado Sauce, Cheesy Lasagne Pizza.

CREAMY MUSHROOM AND BACON PASTA SAUCE

½lb pasta twists
1 tablespoon olive oil
1 onion, finely chopped
½lb slices bacon, thinly sliced
3 tablespoons pine nuts
½lb button mushrooms, thinly sliced
½ cup sour cream
1 egg, lightly beaten
¼ cup grated fresh Parmesan cheese
¼ cup chopped fresh parsley

Add pasta to large pan of boiling water, boil, uncovered, until just tender, drain.

Heat oil in pan, add onion, bacon and pine nuts, cook, stirring, until onion is soft. Add mushrooms, cook, stirring, until mushrooms are soft. Stir in combined sour cream, egg, cheese and parsley, stir over low heat until heated through. Serve over pasta.

Serves 4.

■ Recipe best made just before serving.
■ Freeze: Not suitable.
■ Microwave: Pasta suitable.

VEAL LASAGNE ROLLS

1lb veal steaks, chopped
2 tablespoons olive oil
1 onion, chopped
1 clove garlic, minced
14½oz can tomatoes
1 cup water
3 tablespoons tomato paste
3 tablespoons chopped
   fresh parsley
½lb instant lasagne pasta sheets

WHITE WINE SAUCE
2 tablespoons (¼ stick) butter
2 tablespoons all-purpose flour
1 cup milk
¼ cup dry white wine
½ cup grated cheddar cheese
3 tablespoons chopped
   fresh parsley
2 tablespoons chopped
   drained capers
3 anchovy fillets, drained, chopped

Process veal until fine. Heat oil in pan, add onion and garlic, cook, stirring, until onion is soft. Add veal, cook, stirring, until browned. Stir in undrained crushed tomatoes, water, paste and parsley. Simmer, uncovered, about 30 minutes or until thickened. Allow mixture to cool for 5 minutes, blend or process until smooth.

Place pasta sheets into pan of boiling water in batches, remove pan from heat, stand 5 minutes or until pliable; drain on absorbent paper.

Divide filling evenly over pasta sheets, roll up firmly. Place rolls in single layer in greased ovenproof dish, cover with sauce, bake, uncovered, in 350°F oven about 30 minutes or until rolls are tender.

White Wine Sauce: Melt butter in pan, add flour, stir over heat until bubbling. Remove from heat, gradually stir in milk and wine. Stir over heat until sauce boils and thickens. Remove from heat, stir in cheese, parsley, capers and anchovies.

Serves 6.

■ Recipe can be made a day ahead.
■ Storage: Covered, in refrigerator.
■ Freeze: Uncooked rolls suitable.
■ Microwave: Sauce suitable.

BAKED PASTA FRITTATA WITH TOMATO WINE SAUCE

1½ cups (10oz) orzo pasta
14½oz can tomatoes
½lb mushrooms, chopped
7oz salami, chopped
½ cup grated cheddar cheese
4 eggs, lightly beaten
¼ cup chopped fresh parsley
½ cup packaged unseasoned
   bread crumbs
½ cup grated fresh Parmesan cheese

TOMATO WINE SAUCE
½ cup water
¼ cup dry white wine
3 tablespoons tomato paste
3 tablespoons chopped fresh parsley

Lightly grease deep 9 inch round baking pan. Add pasta to large pan of boiling water, boil, uncovered, until just tender; drain well.

Drain and chop tomatoes; reserve liquid for sauce. Combine tomatoes, mushrooms, salami, cheddar cheese, eggs, parsley and pasta in bowl; mix well.

Combine bread crumbs and Parmesan cheese, add half to prepared pan, shake crumb mixture around base and side to coat evenly. Spoon pasta mixture into pan, press lightly, sprinkle with remaining crumb mixture.

Just before serving, bake in 350°F oven about 40 minutes or until well browned. Stand 5 minutes before turning out and cutting; serve with sauce.

Tomato Wine Sauce: Combine reserved tomato liquid with remaining ingredients in pan. Simmer, uncovered, about 15 minutes or until thickened.

Serves 6.

■ Recipe can be prepared
   6 hours ahead.
■ Storage: Covered, in refrigerator.
■ Freeze: Not suitable.
■ Microwave: Pasta suitable.

LEFT: Clockwise from left: Veal Lasagne Rolls, Creamy Mushroom and Bacon Pasta Sauce, Baked Pasta Frittata with Tomato Wine Sauce.

VEAL AND CHEESE BALLS WITH BASIL CREAM SAUCE

⅔ quantity herbed pasta dough
1lb veal steaks, chopped
½ cup grated fresh Parmesan cheese
½ cup fresh bread crumbs
1 egg, lightly beaten
3 tablespoons chopped fresh basil
2oz mozzarella cheese
all-purpose flour
2 tablespoons (¼ stick) butter
1 tablespoon olive oil

BASIL CREAM SAUCE
2 tablespoons (¼ stick) butter
1 onion, chopped
¼ cup chopped fresh basil
½ cup heavy cream
1 tablespoon cornstarch
½ cup water

Roll pasta dough until ⅛ inch thick, cut into 1 inch x 12 inch strips.

Process veal until ground, add Parmesan cheese, bread crumbs, egg and basil, process until combined. Cut mozzarella cheese into small cubes. Shape 1 rounded tablespoon of veal mixture around a mozzarella cube, roll into meatball; repeat with remaining veal mixture and mozzarella cubes. Toss meatballs lightly in flour, shake away excess flour.

Heat butter and oil in pan, add meatballs, cook until meatballs are well browned. Transfer meatballs to roasting pan, bake, covered, in 350°F oven about 10 minutes or until cooked through.

Add pasta to large pan of boiling water, boil, uncovered, until just tender; drain. Serve meatballs with pasta and sauce.

Basil Cream Sauce: Melt butter in pan, add onion, cook, stirring, until soft. Add basil, cream, blended cornstarch and water, stir until sauce boils and thickens.

Serves 4.

■ Meatballs and sauce can be made a day ahead.
■ Storage: Covered, in refrigerator.
■ Freeze: Meatballs suitable.
■ Microwave: Pasta and sauce suitable.

SPICY TORTELLINI SALAD

1lb pork and veal tortellini
2 carrots
1 red bell pepper
1 green bell pepper
½lb button mushrooms, chopped
¼ cup pitted black olives, sliced

PESTO DRESSING
¼ cup olive oil
¼ cup white vinegar
2 cloves garlic, minced
¼ cup chopped fresh basil
3 tablespoons grated
    Parmesan cheese
2 tablespoons tomato paste

Add tortellini to large pan of boiling water, boil, uncovered, until just tender; drain. Rinse tortellini under cold water; drain.

Cut carrots and peppers into thin strips. Combine tortellini, uncooked vegetables and olives in bowl, pour over dressing.

Pesto Dressing: Combine all ingredients in bowl; mix well.

Serves 4.

■ Salad can be made a day ahead.
■ Storage: Covered, in refrigerator.
■ Freeze: Not suitable.
■ Microwave: Tortellini suitable.

CREAMY BACON AND BASIL TAGLIATELLE

1lb tagliatelle pasta
1 tablespoon olive oil

SAUCE
½lb slices bacon, thinly sliced
1¼ cups heavy cream
⅓ cup dry white wine
2 teaspoons seeded mustard
3 tablespoons grated fresh
    Parmesan cheese
1 tablespoon cornstarch
2 tablespoons water
½ cup chopped fresh basil
6 green onions, chopped

Add pasta to large pan of boiling water, boil, uncovered, until just tender; drain. Combine pasta and oil. Serve pasta topped with sauce.

Sauce: Cook bacon in pan until crisp. Stir in cream, wine, mustard, cheese and blended cornstarch and water. Stir over heat until sauce boils and thickens. Stir in basil and onions.

Serves 4.

■ Sauce can be made a day ahead.
■ Storage: Covered, in refrigerator.
■ Freeze: Not suitable.
■ Microwave: Pasta suitable.

LEFT: Veal and Cheese Balls with Basil Cream Sauce.
RIGHT: From back: Spicy Tortellini Salad, Creamy Bacon and Basil Tagliatelle.

HOT SPICY RAVIOLI WITH GARBANZO SALAD

1 quantity chili pasta dough
all-purpose flour
1 red bell pepper
1 green bell pepper
15oz can garbanzo beans,
    rinsed, drained

FILLING
2 tablespoons (¼ stick) butter
1 onion, chopped
1 teaspoon white mustard seeds
1 clove garlic, minced
5oz chorizo sausage, chopped

DRESSING
⅓ cup olive oil
3 tablespoons lemon juice
½ teaspoon sugar
2 green onions, chopped

Cut pasta dough in half, roll each half to a ⅛ inch thick rectangle. Place ¼ level teaspoons of filling 1¼ inches apart over 1 sheet of pasta. Lightly brush remaining pasta sheet with water, place over filling; press firmly between filling. Cut into square ravioli shapes; lightly sprinkle with flour.

Add ravioli to large pan of boiling water, boil, uncovered, about 5 minutes or until just tender; drain. Rinse ravioli under cold water, drain; cool.

Quarter peppers, remove seeds and membrane, broil, skin-side-up, until skin blackens and blisters. Peel skin, cut peppers into thin strips.

Combine ravioli, peppers, beans and dressing in bowl; mix well.
Filling: Melt butter in pan, add onion, mustard seeds and garlic, cook, stirring, until onion is soft. Blend or process onion mixture and sausage until finely chopped.
Dressing: Combine all ingredients in jar; shake well.

Serves 6.

■ Salad can be made 2 hours ahead.
■ Storage: Covered, in refrigerator.
■ Freeze: Uncooked ravioli suitable.
■ Microwave: Not suitable.

CANNELLONI SALAD WITH CUCUMBER YOGURT DRESSING

¼lb cannelloni pasta
2 hard-boiled eggs
1 cup (¼lb) grated cheddar cheese
¼lb cherry tomatoes, quartered
3 pitted black olives, chopped
5 slices cooked ham, chopped
2 green onions, chopped
lettuce leaves

CUCUMBER YOGURT DRESSING
2 small green cucumbers,
    peeled, chopped
1 cup plain yogurt
2 tablespoons chopped fresh chives

Add pasta to large pan of boiling water, boil, uncovered, until just tender; drain. Rinse pasta under cold water; drain.

Push eggs through sieve, combine with cheese, tomatoes, olives, ham and onions. Carefully spoon egg mixture into pasta. Serve pasta on lettuce leaves with dressing.
Cucumber Yogurt Dressing: Blend or process cucumbers until smooth, add yogurt, blend until combined; stir in chives.
Serves 6.

■ Salad can be made 6 hours ahead.
■ Storage: Covered, in refrigerator.
■ Freeze: Not suitable.
■ Microwave: Suitable.

PORK AND EGG SALAD WITH CHICKEN AND CHEESE

1lb pasta crests
7oz snow peas
1 cup (5oz) chopped cooked chicken
4 hard-boiled eggs, halved
7oz barbequed red pork, sliced
1 red bell pepper, chopped
1 stalk celery, sliced
7oz cheddar cheese, chopped
1 romaine lettuce

DRESSING
¼ cup white vinegar
⅓ cup olive oil
3 tablespoons chopped
    fresh chives
1 teaspoon seeded mustard

Add pasta to large pan of boiling water, boil, uncovered, until just tender; drain. Rinse pasta under cold water; drain.

Boil, steam or microwave peas until just tender, rinse under cold water, drain. Combine peas, pasta, chicken, eggs, pork, pepper, celery and cheese in bowl; add dressing, toss lightly. Serve salad on lettuce leaves.
Dressing: Combine all ingredients in jar; shake well.

Serves 8.

■ Salad can be made a day ahead.
■ Storage: Covered, in refrigerator.
■ Freeze: Not suitable.
■ Microwave: Pasta and peas suitable.

PEPPERED PASTA WITH PROSCIUTTO

5oz angels' hair pasta
1 large lemon
1 orange
5oz thinly sliced prosciutto
¼ cup olive oil
2 cloves garlic, minced
4 green onions, finely chopped
½ cup drained sun-dried
    tomatoes, sliced
⅓ cup finely grated fresh
    Parmesan cheese
1 teaspoon cracked black
    peppercorns
2 tablespoons chopped fresh
    lemon thyme

Add pasta to large pan of boiling water, boil, uncovered, until just tender; drain. Rinse pasta under cold water; drain.

Using vegetable peeler, thinly cut peel from lemon and orange, avoiding white pith; cut peel into thin strips. Add strips to pan of boiling water, boil 1 minute; drain. Cut prosciutto into ½ inch ribbons.

Heat oil in pan, add garlic and half the onions, cook, stirring, until onions are soft. Add prosciutto and peel, cook, stirring, until prosciutto is lightly browned; cool.

Combine pasta, prosciutto mixture, tomatoes, cheese, peppercorns and thyme in bowl; cover, refrigerate several hours. Sprinkle with remaining onions before serving.

Serves 4.

■ Recipe can be made a day ahead.
■ Storage: Covered, in refrigerator.
■ Freeze: Not suitable.
■ Microwave: Pasta and peel suitable.

LEFT: Clockwise from back: Peppered Pasta with Prosciutto, Cannelloni Salad with Cucumber Yogurt Dressing, Hot Spicy Ravioli with Garbanzo Salad, Pork and Egg Salad with Chicken and Cheese.

VEGETARIAN

You'll find inspiration here with the fresh, healthy appeal of vegetables adding to the pleasures of pasta in main courses and side dishes. For example, salads include an unusual fried tofu salad and a potato salad with a difference. Macaroni, so familiar, takes on new flair in our cheese sauce pie or nutty macaroni loaf. And among other favorites to sample are mushrooms, especially delicious in our double mushroom ravioli with burnt butter, and cheese and mushroom lasagne.

CHEESE TORTELLINI SALAD WITH MUSTARD MAYONNAISE

½lb cheese tortellini
1 bunch (½lb) fresh asparagus, chopped
7oz green beans, chopped
1 small red bell pepper
1 small green bell pepper
¼lb button mushrooms, chopped
4 green onions, chopped

MUSTARD MAYONNAISE
2 egg yolks
1 tablespoon lemon juice
¾ cup olive oil
1 tablespoon seeded mustard
1 clove garlic, minced
2 teaspoons water

Add tortellini to pan of boiling water, boil, uncovered, until just tender, drain; cool.

Boil or steam asparagus and beans until just tender; drain, rinse under cold water. Cut peppers into thin strips. Combine tortellini, vegetables and onions in bowl. Refrigerate several hours before serving with mustard mayonnaise.
Mustard Mayonnaise: Blend or process egg yolks and juice until pale and thick. With motor operating, gradually pour in oil in a thin stream; blend until thick. Stir in mustard, garlic and water.

Serves 4.
■ Salad can be made a day ahead.
■ Storage: Covered, in refrigerator.
■ Freeze: Not suitable.
■ Microwave: Vegetables suitable.

SPICY VEGETABLE STIR-FRY WITH PASTA

⅓ cup olive oil
1 onion, sliced
1 green bell pepper, chopped
1 medium eggplant, chopped
2 large tomatoes, peeled, chopped
1 stalk celery, sliced
2 vegetable bouillon cubes, crumbled
½ teaspoon dried thyme leaves
2 bay leaves
1 tablespoon sambal oelek
½ cup water
½ cup dry red wine
7oz snow peas, sliced
⅔ cup black olives
2 green onions, chopped
¾lb penne pasta

Heat oil in pan, add onion and pepper, cook, stirring, until onion is soft. Stir in eggplant and tomatoes, cook over low heat 5 minutes. Add celery, bouillon cubes, thyme, bay leaves, sambal oelek, water and wine. Bring to boil, simmer, uncovered, 10 minutes. Stir in peas, olives and green onions; keep warm. Discard bay leaves.

Add pasta to large pan of boiling water, boil, uncovered, until just tender; drain.
Just before serving, toss pasta with vegetable mixture.
Serves 6.
■ Recipe best made just before serving.
■ Freeze: Not suitable.
■ Microwave: Pasta suitable.

TOMATOES AND BLACK BEAN PASTA SAUCE

1lb pasta twists
¼ cup olive oil
3 small fresh red chili peppers, chopped
3 cloves garlic, minced
⅓ cup drained sliced sun-dried tomatoes
3 green onions, sliced
3 tablespoons chopped fresh basil
½ teaspoon ground gingerroot
¼ cup packaged salted black beans, chopped
14½oz can tomatoes
¼ cup tomato paste
⅔ cup water
½ teaspoon Vecon paste
2 green onions, chopped, extra

Add pasta to large pan of boiling water, boil, uncovered, until just tender, drain.

Heat oil in wok or pan, add chilies, garlic, sun-dried tomatoes, onions, basil, gingerroot and beans, stir-fry 1 minute. Add pasta, stir-fry until hot.

Blend or process undrained canned tomatoes until smooth, add to wok with paste, water and Vecon, stir-fry until hot. Serve sprinkled with extra onions.
Serves 4.
■ Recipe best made close to serving.
■ Freeze: Not suitable.
■ Microwave: Pasta suitable.

RIGHT: Clockwise from front: Tomatoes and Black Bean Pasta Sauce, Cheese Tortellini Salad with Mustard Mayonnaise, Spicy Vegetable Stir-Fry with Pasta.

EGGPLANT, TOMATO AND FETA CHEESE SALAD

¼lb penne pasta
1 large (about 1lb) eggplant, chopped
salt
¼ cup olive oil
1 onion, finely chopped
2 cloves garlic, minced
2 x 14½oz cans tomatoes
⅓ cup tomato paste
2 teaspoons vinegar
1 tablespoon sugar
1 teaspoon dried oregano leaves
¼ cup black olives
7oz feta cheese, chopped
4 green onions, chopped

Add pasta to large pan of boiling water, boil, uncovered, until just tender; drain. Rinse pasta under cold water; drain.

Sprinkle eggplant with salt in bowl, stand for 30 minutes.

Rinse eggplant under cold water; drain well. Heat oil in pan, add onion and garlic, cook, stirring, until onion is soft. Add undrained crushed tomatoes, paste, vinegar, sugar and oregano. Simmer, uncovered, until slightly thickened; cool. Stir in pasta, eggplant, olives, cheese and onions; mix well. Serve warm or cold.

Serves 4.
■ Salad can be made a day ahead.
■ Storage: Covered, in refrigerator.
■ Freeze: Not suitable.
■ Microwave: Pasta suitable.

POTATO AND PASTA SALAD WITH OLIVE VINAIGRETTE

1½lb potatoes
2 cups (¾lb) orzo pasta
2 tablespoons olive oil
2 teaspoons black mustard seeds
1 onion, chopped
1 clove garlic, minced
¾ teaspoon ground cumin
1 small green bell pepper, thinly sliced
1 small red bell pepper, thinly sliced
2 tablespoons chopped fresh parsley

OLIVE VINAIGRETTE
½ cup pimiento-stuffed olives
⅓ cup fresh orange juice
⅓ cup olive oil

Cut potatoes into ¾ inch cubes. Boil, steam or microwave potatoes until almost tender; drain, spread onto tray to cool.

Add pasta to large pan of boiling water, boil, uncovered, until just tender; drain. Rinse pasta under cold water; drain.

Heat oil in pan, add seeds, cook, stirring, until seeds begin to pop. Add onion and garlic, cook, stirring, until onion is soft; stir in cumin. Add potato, cook, stirring gently, until potato is lightly browned and tender; cool.

Combine potato mixture, pasta, peppers and parsley in bowl. Pour olive vinaigrette over potato mixture; mix gently.
Olive Vinaigrette: Blend or process all ingredients until smooth.

Serves 6.
■ Salad can be made a day ahead.
■ Storage: Covered, in refrigerator.
■ Freeze: Not suitable.
■ Microwave: Potatoes and pasta suitable.

PEPPERED PASTA AND CHEESE SALAD

2 cups (5oz) shell pasta
2 red bell peppers
½lb goats' milk cheese, chopped
¼ cup pine nuts, toasted
2 tablespoons small fresh marjoram leaves

DRESSING
3 tablespoons white vinegar
¼ cup olive oil
½ teaspoon cracked black peppercorns

Add pasta to large pan of boiling water, boil, uncovered, until just tender; drain. Rinse pasta under cold water; drain.

Quarter peppers, remove seeds and membrane. Broil peppers, skin-side-up, until skin blisters and blackens; cool slightly. Remove skin, cut peppers into long thin strips.

Combine peppers, pasta, cheese, nuts and marjoram in bowl, pour over dressing; toss well. Serve salad warm or cold.
Dressing: Combine all ingredients in jar; shake well.

Serves 6.
■ Salad can be made a day ahead.
■ Storage: Covered, in refrigerator.
■ Freeze: Not Suitable.
■ Microwave: Pasta suitable.

RIGHT: Clockwise from front: Peppered Pasta and Cheese Salad, Potato and Pasta Salad with Olive Vinaigrette, Eggplant, Tomato and Feta Cheese Salad.

CREAMY LEMON ZUCCHINI PASTA SAUCE

¾lb bow-tie pasta
4 small (about ½lb)
   zucchini, sliced
2 small (about ¼lb) yellow
   squash, sliced
½ cup (1 stick) butter
¼ cup lemon juice
1 cup heavy cream
⅔ cup grated fresh Parmesan cheese
1 teaspoon sugar
2 teaspoons cornstarch
1 tablespoon water
3 green onions, chopped

Add pasta to large pan of boiling water, boil, uncovered, until just tender, drain; keep warm.

Boil, steam or microwave zucchini and squash until just tender. Melt butter in pan, stir in juice, cream, cheese, sugar and blended cornstarch and water, stir over heat until mixture boils and thickens. Stir in onions and zucchini. Serve sauce over warm pasta; sprinkle with extra Parmesan cheese, if desired.

Serves 4.

■ Recipe best made close to serving.
■ Freeze: Not suitable.
■ Microwave: Suitable.

FRESH HERB PASTA WITH HOT 'N' SPICY DRESSING

2 carrots
1lb penne pasta
½ cup chopped fresh basil
½ cup chopped fresh mint
½ cup chopped fresh cilantro
½ cup bean sprouts
2 teaspoons vegetable oil
2 cloves garlic, sliced
3 tablespoons unsalted
   chopped cashews

HOT 'N' SPICY DRESSING
3 tablespoons vegetable oil
¼ cup olive oil
1 teaspoon Oriental sesame oil
¼ cup lime juice
3 tablespoons light soy sauce
½ teaspoon sugar
2 teaspoons sambal oelek (Chillies & Salt Paste)

Cut carrots into thin sticks. Add pasta to large pan of boiling water, boil, uncovered, until just tender; drain.

Combine pasta, carrots, herbs and sprouts in bowl; add dressing, toss well.

Heat oil in pan, add garlic, cook until lightly browned and crisp. Top salad with garlic and nuts.

Hot 'n' Spicy Dressing: Combine all ingredients in jar; shake well.

Serves 6.

■ Salad best made close to serving.
■ Freeze: Not suitable.
■ Microwave: Pasta suitable.

NOODLES AND VEGETABLES WITH SATAY DRESSING

5oz fresh egg noodles
1 teaspoon Oriental sesame oil
15oz can baby corn, drained
3 small green cucumbers, peeled
1 cup (3½oz) bean sprouts

SATAY DRESSING
3 tablespoons smooth peanut butter
3 tablespoons water
3 tablespoons light soy sauce
1 tablespoon Oriental sesame oil
3 tablespoons lime juice
2 teaspoons rice vinegar
2 cloves garlic, minced
2 teaspoons grated fresh gingerroot
1 tablespoon sugar

Add noodles to pan of boiling water, boil, uncovered, until just tender; drain. Toss noodles with oil in bowl.

Cut corn and cucumbers into strips, add to noodles with sprouts. Add dressing, toss well; serve warm or cold.

Satay Dressing: Combine all ingredients in pan, stir over heat until combined and heated through; do not boil.

Serves 6.

■ Recipe can be made a day ahead.
■ Storage: Covered, in refrigerator.
■ Freeze: Not suitable.
■ Microwave: Noodles suitable.

LEFT: Creamy Lemon Zucchini Pasta Sauce.
RIGHT: From left: Fresh Herb Pasta with
Hot 'n' Spicy Dressing, Noodles and
Vegetables with Satay Dressing.

ONION RAVIOLI WITH THYME AND LEMON CREAM

3 tablespoons olive oil
3 red onions, sliced
2 hard-boiled eggs, chopped
½ teaspoon dried thyme leaves
1 quantity plain pasta dough

THYME AND LEMON CREAM
1¼ cups heavy cream
3 tablespoons chopped fresh thyme
½ teaspoon grated lemon zest
2 teaspoons cornstarch
1 tablespoon water

Heat oil in pan, add onions, cook over low heat about 10 minutes or until very soft; cool. Blend or process onions, eggs and thyme until almost smooth.

Cut pasta dough into quarters, roll each quarter until ⅛ inch thick rectangle. Place ½ level teaspoons of filling 1¼ inches apart over 2 of the pasta sheets. Brush remaining pasta sheets with water, place over filling, press firmly between filling and along edges of pasta. Cut into 1¼ inch round ravioli shapes.

Just before serving, add ravioli to large pan of boiling water, boil, uncovered, about 2 minutes or until tender; drain. Serve ravioli with thyme and lemon cream sprinkled with extra thyme, if desired.

Thyme and Lemon Cream: Combine cream, thyme and zest in pan, simmer, uncovered, 5 minutes. Stir in blended cornstarch and water, stir until sauce boils and thickens; strain.

Serves 4.

■ Ravioli can be prepared a day ahead.
■ Storage: Covered, in refrigerator.
■ Freeze: Uncooked ravioli suitable.
■ Microwave: Cream suitable.

THREE CHEESES AND MUSHROOM LASAGNE

1 tablespoon olive oil
1 onion, chopped
2 cloves garlic, minced
1 red bell pepper, chopped
10oz mushrooms, sliced
14½oz can tomatoes
1 tablespoon sugar
¼ cup tomato paste
1 cup water
½ teaspoon Vecon paste
8oz package cream cheese
½lb cottage cheese
½lb spinach lasagne pasta sheets
½ bunch (10oz) spinach
2 cups (½lb) grated cheddar cheese

Lightly grease shallow ovenproof dish (8 cup capacity).

Heat oil in pan, add onion, garlic and pepper, cook, stirring, until onion is soft. Add mushrooms, undrained crushed tomatoes, sugar, paste, water and Vecon. Bring to boil, simmer, uncovered, for about 30 minutes or until mixture is thickened.

Beat cream cheese and cottage cheese in small bowl with electric mixer until smooth.

Add pasta to large pan of boiling water, boil, uncovered, until just tender; drain.

Spread small amount of tomato mixture over base of prepared dish, cover with single layer of pasta. Spread pasta with one-third of cheese mixture, cover with some of the spinach leaves, spread with one-third of tomato mixture. Repeat layering, ending with tomato mixture.

Bake, covered, in 350°F oven 1 hour, sprinkle with cheddar cheese, bake, uncovered, about 20 minutes or until lasagne is lightly browned.

Serves 6.

■ Recipe can be made 2 days ahead.
■ Storage: Covered, in refrigerator.
■ Freeze: Suitable.
■ Microwave: Pasta suitable.

BAKED RED BELL PEPPERS AND GARLIC WITH PASTA

4 large red bell peppers
2 cloves garlic, finely chopped
⅓ cup olive oil
1 tablespoon brown sugar
13oz penne pasta
¼ cup shredded fresh basil

Cut peppers into strips, combine peppers, garlic, oil and sugar in a roasting pan; mix well. Bake pepper mixture in 350°F oven about 1 hour or until peppers are soft.

Add pasta to large pan of boiling water, boil, uncovered, until just tender; drain. Return pasta to pan, stir in pepper mixture and basil.

Serves 4.

■ Recipe best made just before serving.
■ Freeze: Not suitable.
■ Microwave: Pasta suitable.

DEEP-DISH EGGPLANT AND PASTA TORTE

3 large (about 3lb) eggplants
salt
oil
¾lb rigatoni pasta
1 cup tomato-based pasta sauce
3 tablespoons tomato paste
1 cup (3½oz) shredded mozzarella cheese
½ cup grated fresh Parmesan cheese
2 tablespoons chopped fresh basil
2 eggs, lightly beaten
1 tablespoon packaged unseasoned bread crumbs

Grease deep 9 inch round baking pan. Cut eggplants into ⅛ inch slices, place slices on wire rack, sprinkle with salt, stand 20 minutes. Rinse eggplant under cold water; pat dry with absorbent paper.

Heat a little oil in pan, add eggplant slices in single layer, cook until lightly browned on both sides; drain. Repeat with more oil and remaining slices.

Add pasta to large pan of boiling water, boil, uncovered, until just tender; drain.

Combine pasta, sauce, paste, cheeses, basil and eggs in bowl. Center a large eggplant slice in base of prepared pan, reserve about 10 slices for top. Place remaining eggplant slices around center

slice to cover base and side of pan.

Spoon pasta mixture into pan, arrange reserved eggplant slices over top, sprinkle with bread crumbs.

Just before serving, bake in 350°F oven about 30 minutes or until firm. Stand torte 10 minutes before serving.

Serves 6.

■ Recipe can be prepared a day ahead.
■ Storage: Covered, in refrigerator.
■ Freeze: Not suitable.
■ Microwave: Pasta suitable.

ABOVE: Clockwise from back left: Three Cheeses and Mushroom Lasagne, Baked Red Bell Peppers and Garlic with Pasta, Onion Ravioli with Thyme and Lemon Cream, Deep-Dish Eggplant and Pasta Torte.

SPINACH TORTELLINI WITH TOMATO MUSHROOM SAUCE

10oz package frozen chopped spinach, thawed
2 onions, finely chopped
1½ quantities tomato pasta dough
1 egg, lightly beaten

TOMATO MUSHROOM SAUCE
¼ cup olive oil
1 onion, chopped
2 cloves garlic, minced
2 x 14½oz cans tomatoes
½ cup pine nuts
1 cup water
1 tablespoon sugar
5oz mushrooms, chopped
3 tablespoons cornstarch
¼ cup water, extra
½ cup chopped fresh parsley

Squeeze excess moisture from spinach, combine spinach with onions in bowl. Roll pasta dough until ⅛ inch thick, cut into 2 inch rounds. Brush rounds with egg, top each round with ½ level teaspoon of spinach mixture. Fold rounds in half, press edges together, pinch corners together. **Just before serving,** add tortellini to large pan of boiling water, boil, uncovered, about 5 minutes or until tender, drain. Add tortellini to tomato mushroom sauce. Serve with extra parsley, if desired.

Tomato Mushroom Sauce: Heat oil in pan, add onion and garlic, cook, stirring, until onion is soft. Add undrained crushed tomatoes, nuts, water and sugar. Simmer, uncovered, 5 minutes. Add mushrooms, simmer, uncovered, further 10 minutes. Stir in blended cornstarch and extra water, stir until sauce boils and thickens. Stir in parsley; cool.

Serves 4.

- Tortellini and sauce can be made a day ahead.
- Storage: Covered, in refrigerator.
- Freeze: Cooked tortellini and sauce suitable.
- Microwave: Not suitable.

NUTTY MACARONI LOAF WITH YOGURT SAUCE

1 cup (¼lb) small macaroni pasta
1 cup (2½oz) fresh bread crumbs
1 cup (¼lb) ground cashews
1 cup (¼lb) ground brazil nuts
1 cup (2½oz) grated fresh Parmesan cheese
1 cup (¼lb) grated cheddar cheese
3 tablespoons golden raisins
½ teaspoon garam masala
½ teaspoon turmeric
¼ teaspoon ground cumin
1 red bell pepper, finely chopped
3 tablespoons chopped fresh cilantro
5 eggs, lightly beaten

YOGURT SAUCE
1 cup plain yogurt
2 teaspoons chopped fresh cilantro
½ teaspoon garam masala

Grease 5½ inch x 8½ inch loaf pan, line base and sides with paper, grease paper. Add pasta to pan of boiling water, boil, uncovered, until just tender, drain; cool.

Combine pasta, bread crumbs, nuts, cheeses, raisins, spices, pepper, cilantro and eggs in bowl; mix well. Spoon mixture into prepared pan, smooth surface. Bake, uncovered, in 350°F oven about 30 minutes or until firm. Serve loaf hot or cold with sauce.

Yogurt Sauce: Combine all ingredients in bowl; mix well.

Serves 6.

- Recipe can be made 2 days ahead.
- Storage: Covered, in refrigerator.
- Freeze: Cooked loaf suitable.
- Microwave: Pasta suitable.

LEFT: From front: Nutty Macaroni Loaf with Yogurt Sauce, Spinach Tortellini with Tomato Mushroom Sauce.
RIGHT: Double Mushroom Ravioli with Burnt Butter.

DOUBLE MUSHROOM RAVIOLI WITH BURNT BUTTER

⅔ quantity tomato pasta dough
1 egg white, lightly beaten

FILLING
1 tablespoon butter
1 onion, chopped
2 cloves garlic, minced
7oz mushrooms, chopped
7oz shitake mushrooms, chopped
1 tablespoon chopped fresh tarragon

BURNT BUTTER
1 cup (2 sticks) butter
1 tablespoon white vinegar

Cut pasta dough in half, roll each half until ⅛ inch thick rectangle. Place level teaspoons of filling 1¼ inches apart over 1 sheet of pasta. Lightly brush remaining sheet with egg white, place over filling, press firmly between filling and along edges of pasta. Cut into square ravioli shapes; lightly sprinkle ravioli with flour.

Just before serving, add ravioli to large pan of boiling water, boil, uncovered, about 5 minutes or until just tender; drain. Serve ravioli with burnt butter.

Filling: Heat butter in pan, add onion and garlic, cook, stirring, until onion is soft. Add both mushrooms and tarragon, cook, stirring, until mushrooms are just tender.

Burnt Butter: Heat butter in pan until lightly browned, stir in vinegar.

Serves 6.

- Ravioli can be prepared a day ahead. Burnt butter best made just before serving.
- Storage: Covered, in refrigerator.
- Freeze: Not suitable.
- Microwave: Burnt butter suitable.

NO-COOK TOMATO ONION SAUCE WITH FRESH HERBS

1 red onion, finely chopped
2 large tomatoes, peeled, seeded, chopped
1 clove garlic, minced
2 tablespoons lemon juice
¼ cup olive oil
1 teaspoon chopped fresh lemon thyme
½ teaspoon cracked black peppercorns
10oz pasta twists
2 tablespoons shredded fresh basil

Cover onion with water in bowl, stand 1 hour; drain. Combine tomatoes with onion, garlic, juice, oil, thyme and peppercorns in bowl; cover, refrigerate 1 hour.
Just before serving, add pasta to large pan of boiling water, boil, uncovered, until just tender; drain. Serve cold tomato onion juice with pasta. Serve cold tomato onion sauce over hot pasta, sprinkle with basil.
Serves 4.

■ Sauce can be made a day ahead.
■ Storage: Covered, in refrigerator.
■ Freeze: Not suitable.
■ Microwave: Pasta suitable.

MACARONI AND SUN-DRIED TOMATO SALAD WITH PESTO

2 cups (½lb) macaroni pasta
5oz snow peas
5oz button mushrooms, halved
1 red bell pepper, finely chopped
½ cup drained sun-dried tomatoes, sliced

PESTO
1 bunch fresh basil
4 cloves garlic, minced
3 tablespoons lemon juice
¾ cup olive oil
1 cup (3½oz) grated pecorino cheese

Add pasta to large pan of boiling water, boil, uncovered, until just tender; drain. Rinse pasta under cold water; drain.

Boil, steam or microwave snow peas and mushrooms until just tender, rinse under cold water; drain. Combine pasta, vegetables, tomatoes and pesto in bowl, mix well; cover, refrigerate 1 hour before serving. Serve with lettuce, if desired.
Pesto: Blend or process basil leaves, garlic and juice until combined, gradually add oil in thin stream while motor is operating. Add cheese, process until combined.
Serves 6.

■ Salad can be made a day ahead.
■ Storage: Covered, in refrigerator.
■ Freeze: Not suitable.
■ Microwave: Suitable.

LEFT: No-Cook Tomato Onion Sauce with Fresh Herbs.
ABOVE: Macaroni and Sun-Dried Tomato Salad with Pesto.

FRIED TOFU SALAD WITH CREAMY VEGETABLES

¾ cup mini bow-tie pasta
2 carrots, grated
2 small zucchini, grated
2 stalks celery, chopped
1 red bell pepper, chopped
1 large tomato, chopped
¼ cup olive oil
5oz firm tofu, cubed
1½ teaspoons cuminseed
2 teaspoons white mustard seeds
¼ cup olive oil, extra
1 small fresh red chili pepper, chopped
1 medium (about 10oz) eggplant, cubed
1 cup plain yogurt

Add pasta to large pan of boiling water, boil, uncovered, until just tender; drain. Rinse pasta under cold water; drain.

Combine pasta, carrots, zucchini, celery, pepper and tomato in bowl. Heat oil in pan, add tofu, cook, stirring gently, until browned, drain on absorbent paper. Add tofu to vegetable mixture.

Heat a dry pan, add cuminseed and mustard seeds, cook, stirring, until seeds pop. Add extra oil, chili and eggplant, cook, stirring, until eggplant is soft. Remove from heat, stir into vegetable mixture. Add yogurt; mix well. Serve salad on lettuce, if desired.

Serves 6.

■ Recipe can be made a day ahead.
■ Storage: Covered, in refrigerator.
■ Freeze: Not suitable.
■ Microwave: Pasta suitable.

MACARONI CHEESE SAUCE PIE

2 cups (7oz) pasta elbows
1½ tablespoons olive oil
1 small onion, chopped
1 clove garlic, minced
1 small red bell pepper, sliced
½ cup canned drained whole-kernel corn
2 zucchini, sliced
1 sheet frozen ready rolled puff pastry, thawed
1 egg yolk

CHEESE SAUCE
3 tablespoons butter
3 tablespoons all-purpose flour
1⅔ cups milk
1 cup (2½oz) grated fresh Parmesan cheese
1 cup (¼lb) grated cheddar cheese
3 tablespoons chopped fresh parsley

Lightly grease deep-sided ovenproof dish (8 cup capacity).

Add pasta to large pan of boiling water, boil, uncovered, until just tender; drain. Rinse pasta under hot water; drain.

Heat oil in pan, add onion, garlic and pepper, cook, stirring, until onion is soft. Combine onion mixture, pasta, corn, zucchini and cheese sauce in bowl; mix well.

Spoon mixture into prepared dish.

Brush pastry with egg yolk, cut into ½ inch strips. Place strips over filling in lattice pattern, press gently against edge of dish; trim edges. Bake pie in 375°F oven about 15 minutes or until pastry is well browned.
Cheese Sauce: Melt butter in pan, stir in flour, stir over heat until bubbling. Remove from heat, gradually stir in milk, stir over heat until sauce boils and thickens slightly. Stir in cheeses and parsley.

Serves 6.

■ Pie can be made a day ahead.
■ Storage: Covered, in refrigerator.
■ Freeze: Cooked pie suitable.
■ Microwave: Pasta and sauce suitable.

PASTA WITH RED BELL PEPPER AND CHILI SAUCE

1lb pipe rigate pasta
3 tablespoons grated Parmesan cheese

RED BELL PEPPER AND CHILI SAUCE
2 red bell peppers
¼ cup drained chopped sun-dried tomatoes
1 small fresh red chili pepper, chopped
2 cloves garlic, minced
1 teaspoon chopped fresh thyme
2 tablespoons tomato paste
¼ cup olive oil
½ teaspoon cracked black peppercorns

Add pasta to large pan of boiling water, boil, uncovered, until just tender, drain; keep warm. Add sauce to pasta, sprinkle with cheese.
Red Bell Pepper and Chili Sauce: Quarter peppers, remove membrane and seeds. Broil peppers, skin-side-up, until skin blisters and blackens; cool. Remove skin, chop peppers roughly.

Blend or process peppers with tomatoes, chili, garlic, thyme, paste, oil and peppercorns until smooth.

Serves 4.

■ Sauce can be made a day ahead.
■ Storage: Covered, in refrigerator.
■ Freeze: Not suitable.
■ Microwave: Pasta suitable.

LEFT: Clockwise from front: Fried Tofu Salad with Creamy Vegetables, Pasta with Red Bell Pepper and Chili Sauce, Macaroni Cheese Sauce Pie.

DESSERTS

Although it sounds unusual to use pasta in sweet ways, you'll enjoy the interesting difference and appeal it adds to these very good desserts. Think of crisp cannelloni shells with creamy coconut ricotta filling, marzipan-filled ravioli with mocha sauce, and lasagne-based apple and almond custard flan. There are other luscious custards and creams, too, variously flavored with caramel, fruit, nuts and spices. Quick ideas include apple butterscotch sauce and easy peanut honey sauce. We've even made chocolate pasta, and lavished it with raspberry sauce!

COCONUT CANNELLONI SNAPS WITH KIWIFRUIT SAUCE

18 cannelloni pasta
oil for deep-frying

KIWIFRUIT SAUCE
4 kiwifruit, peeled
3 tablespoons confectioners' sugar

FILLING
½lb ricotta cheese
3 tablespoons coconut, toasted
2 tablespoons Malibu
¼ cup confectioners' sugar

Add pasta to large pan of boiling water, boil, uncovered, until just tender; drain. Pat pasta dry with absorbent paper. Deep-fry pasta in batches in hot oil until lightly browned; drain on absorbent paper.
Just before serving, spoon filling into piping bag fitted with ¼ inch plain tube, pipe filling into cannelloni, serve cannelloni with sauce.
Kiwifruit Sauce: Blend or process kiwifruit and sifted confectioners' sugar until smooth; push through fine sieve.
Filling: Combine all ingredients in bowl; mix well.
Serves 6.
- Recipe can be prepared a day ahead.
- Storage: Cannelloni shells, in airtight container. Filling and sauce, covered, in refrigerator.
- Freeze: Not suitable.
- Microwave: Pasta suitable.

SWEET PINK PASTA WITH WHITE CHOCOLATE SAUCE

1 cup all-purpose flour
3 tablespoons confectioners' sugar
1 egg, lightly beaten
red food coloring

WHITE CHOCOLATE SAUCE
½ cup milk
½ cup heavy cream
½lb white chocolate, grated
2 teaspoons Kahlua
pinch ground nutmeg

Combine sifted flour and confectioners' sugar with egg and a tiny drop of coloring in food processor. Process until mixture forms a ball. Knead dough on lightly floured surface until smooth and evenly colored; knead in more coloring, if desired.

Roll dough through pasta machine on thickest setting, fold in half, repeat several times. Roll dough until ¹⁄₁₆ inch thick using pasta machine. Cut into strips using fettuccine attachment on machine.

Add pasta to large pan of boiling water, boil, uncovered, about 5 minutes or until just tender; drain. Serve warm pasta with warm sauce.

White Chocolate Sauce: Heat milk and cream in pan, do not boil. Remove from heat, add chocolate, stir until melted, stir in liqueur and nutmeg.
Serves 4.
- Pasta and sauce can be made a day ahead.
- Storage: Covered, in refrigerator.
- Freeze: Not suitable.
- Microwave: Pasta suitable.

RIGHT: From back: Coconut Cannelloni Snaps with Kiwifruit Sauce, Sweet Pink Pasta with White Chocolate Sauce.

EASY PEANUT HONEY SAUCE WITH RICE NOODLES

½ cup smooth peanut butter
½ cup warm water
¼ cup superfine sugar
2 tablespoons honey
7oz rice vermicelli noodles
oil for deep-frying

Blend or process peanut butter, water, sugar and honey until smooth.

Deep-fry noodles in batches in hot oil about 10 seconds or until crisp; drain on absorbent paper. Serve sauce over noodles; top with mango slices, if desired.

Serves 4.

■ Sauce can be made several days ahead. Noodles best cooked just before serving.
■ Freeze: Not suitable.
■ Microwave: Not suitable.

APPLE AND ALMOND CUSTARD FLAN

2 cups milk
¼ cup custard powder
3 tablespoons superfine sugar
½ cup milk, extra
14oz can pie apples
⅓ cup golden raisins
3 tablespoons dark brown sugar
3 tablespoons packaged ground almonds
2 teaspoons all-purpose flour
½ teaspoon ground cinnamon
¼ teaspoon ground nutmeg
pinch ground cloves
1 quantity plain pasta dough
3 tablespoons slivered almonds
confectioners' sugar

Line base and side of 8 inch x 3 inch springform pan with foil; grease foil. Bring milk to boil in pan, stir in blended custard powder, superfine sugar and extra milk, stir until custard boils and thickens; cool.

Combine apples, raisins, dark brown sugar, ground almonds, flour and spices in bowl; mix well.

Roll pasta until ⅛ inch thick, cut into 3 rounds the same size as the prepared pan. Spread a little apple mixture over base of pan, spread with ¼ cup custard; top with a round of pasta.

Spread half the remaining apple mixture over pasta, then one-third of the remaining custard mixture. Repeat layering, finishing with a custard layer. Sprinkle custard with slivered almonds. Bake flan in 350°F oven about 30 minutes or until set; cool. Serve flan hot or cold, sprinkled with sifted confectioners' sugar.

Serves 6 to 8.

■ Recipe can be made a day ahead.
■ Storage: Covered, in refrigerator.
■ Freeze: Not suitable.
■ Microwave: Not suitable.

DATE AND NUT TORTELLINI WITH CUSTARD

⅓ cup chopped pitted dates
1 tablespoon Creme de Cacao
1½oz white chocolate, melted
2½oz packaged cream cheese, softened
¼ teaspoon ground cinnamon
⅓ cup chopped roasted hazelnuts
½ quantity plain pasta dough
1 egg, lightly beaten
14oz can stoneless black cherries, drained

CUSTARD
3 egg yolks
¼ cup superfine sugar
1¼ cups whipping cream
1 tablespoon Kirsch

Combine dates and liqueur in bowl; cover, stand 1 hour.

Blend or process date mixture, chocolate, cheese and cinnamon until smooth; stir in nuts.

Cut pasta dough in half, roll each half until 1/16 inch thick, cut into 3¼ inch rounds. Top each round with 1 level teaspoon of date mixture, brush edges of rounds with water, fold in half, pressing edges to seal. Brush corners with water, pinch together. Lightly sprinkle tortellini with extra flour.

Add pasta to large pan of boiling water, boil, uncovered, until just tender; drain.

Just before serving, place tortellini on lightly greased baking sheet, brush with egg, bake in 400°F oven about 15 minutes or until lightly browned. Serve hot with cherries and custard.

Custard: Beat egg yolks and sugar in small bowl with electric mixer until thick and pale. Heat cream in pan until bubbles appear, do not boil. Whisk egg yolk mixture into cream, stir over heat, without boiling, until mixture thickens slightly, stir in liqueur; mix well.

Serves 6 to 8.

■ Tortellini can be prepared a day ahead. Custard can be made a day ahead.
■ Storage: Covered, in refrigerator.
■ Freeze: Uncooked tortellini suitable.
■ Microwave: Not suitable.

LEFT: From front: Apple and Almond Custard Flan, Easy Peanut Honey Sauce with Rice Noodles.
BELOW: Date and Nut Tortellini with Custard.

CARAMEL RAISIN CUSTARD WITH PEARS

2/3 cup small macaroni pasta
2 cups milk
1/3 cup golden raisins
1/3 cup caramel ice cream topping
2 eggs, separated
4 canned drained pear halves, sliced

Combine pasta and milk in pan, simmer, uncovered, 10 minutes, stirring occasionally. Transfer mixture to bowl; cool to room temperature.

Add raisins, topping and egg yolks to pasta mixture; mix well.

Beat egg whites in small bowl with electric mixer until soft peaks form, gently fold into pasta mixture.

Divide mixture between 4 ovenproof dishes (3/4 cup capacity), top with pears. Cover dishes, place dishes in roasting pan, pour enough boiling water into pan to come halfway up sides of dishes. Bake in 350°F oven about 25 minutes or until firm.

Serves 4.

MARZIPAN RAVIOLI WITH MOCHA SAUCE

1 cup all-purpose flour
¼ cup confectioners' sugar
1 egg, lightly beaten
1 teaspoon water, approximately
1 square (1oz) milk chocolate, melted
3 tablespoons sliced almonds, toasted

FILLING
3½oz prepared marzipan, chopped
2 squares (2 oz) milk chocolate, grated
2 teaspoons water

MOCHA SAUCE
1¼ cups whipping cream
2 teaspoons dry instant coffee
3 tablespoons superfine sugar
1 teaspoon cornstarch
½ cup milk
¼ cup Kahlua

Sift flour and confectioners' sugar into bowl, gradually stir in egg and enough water to mix to a firm dough. Process mixture for 30 seconds or turn onto lightly floured surface and knead gently about 3 minutes or until mixture is well combined, adding a little water if necessary (mixture should be dry, but not flaky).

Cut pasta dough in half, roll each half until ¹⁄₁₆ inch thick rectangle. Place ¼ level teaspoons of filling 1¼ inches apart over 1 sheet of pasta. Lightly brush remaining sheet with water, place over filling; press firmly between filling and along edges. Cut into square ravioli shapes between filling. Lightly sprinkle ravioli with a little extra flour.

Just before serving, add ravioli to large pan of boiling water, boil, uncovered, about 5 minutes or until tender; drain. Serve warm ravioli with warm mocha sauce, drizzle with chocolate and sprinkle with almonds.

Filling: Beat all ingredients in small bowl with electric mixer until smooth.

Mocha Sauce: Combine cream, coffee and sugar in pan. Stir in blended cornstarch and milk, stir over heat until sauce boils and thickens; stir in liqueur.

Serves 6.

■ Ravioli can be made 2 days ahead. Sauce can be made 3 hours ahead.
■ Storage: Covered, in refrigerator.
■ Freeze: Not suitable.
■ Microwave: Sauce suitable.

BAKED PEACH AND PECAN CRUMBLES

1½ cups (¼lb) pasta twists
3 peaches, peeled, sliced
1 teaspoon grated orange zest
⅓ cup fresh orange juice
2 tablespoons water
1 stick cinnamon
3 tablespoons dark brown sugar
2 teaspoons arrowroot
2 teaspoons water, extra
½ cup fresh bread crumbs
¼ cup chopped glace gingerroot
¼ teaspoon mixed spice
½ cup chopped pecans
¼ cup dark brown sugar, extra
2 tablespoons (¼ stick) butter, melted

SPICED CREAM
1 cup whipping cream
2 teaspoons superfine sugar
¼ teaspoon mixed spice

Add pasta to large pan of boiling water, boil, uncovered, until just tender; drain.

Combine peaches, zest, juice, water, cinnamon and sugar in pan, stir over heat until sugar is dissolved. Simmer, covered, about 10 minutes or until peaches are soft; remove cinnamon stick. Stir in blended arrowroot and extra water, stir over high heat until mixture boils and thickens; cool.

Grease 4 ovenproof dishes (1 cup capacity), sprinkle with bread crumbs. Divide half the pasta between dishes; top with peach mixture and gingerroot. Divide remaining pasta between dishes, sprinkle with combined spice, nuts and extra sugar.

Just before serving, drizzle butter over crumbles, place dishes on baking sheet, bake in 350°F oven about 25 minutes or until well browned. Serve warm with spiced cream.

Spiced Cream: Beat all ingredients in small bowl with electric mixer until soft peaks form.

Serves 4.

■ Crumbles can be prepared a day ahead. Spiced cream best prepared just before serving.
■ Storage: Covered, in refrigerator.
■ Freeze: Not suitable.
■ Microwave: Pasta suitable.

■ Recipe best made just before serving.
■ Freeze: Not suitable.
■ Microwave: Not suitable.

LEFT: Clockwise from front: Marzipan Ravioli with Mocha Sauce, Caramel Raisin Custard with Pears, Baked Peach and Pecan Crumbles.

CARAMEL CREAM CUSTARDS

½ cup pasta twists
¾ cup superfine sugar
½ cup water

CUSTARD
6 eggs
1 teaspoon ground cinnamon
⅓ cup superfine sugar
1¼ cups whipping cream
1 cup milk

Add pasta to large pan of boiling water, boil, uncovered, until just tender; drain.

Combine sugar and water in pan, stir over heat until sugar is dissolved. Bring to boil, boil, uncovered, without stirring, about 5 minutes or until golden brown.

Pour toffee over bases of 6 ovenproof molds (¾ cup capacity). Toffee will set at this stage. Spoon pasta into molds, pour custard over pasta.

Place molds in roasting pan, pour in enough boiling water to come halfway up sides of molds. Bake, uncovered, in 350°F oven about 40 minutes or until custard is just set. Remove molds from pan, cool, cover, refrigerate overnight.

Just before serving, run a thin-bladed knife around edge of each mold, turn custards onto plates. Serve with blanched orange peel strips, if desired.

Custard: Whisk eggs, cinnamon and sugar together in bowl. Combine cream and milk in pan, bring to boil. Gradually whisk milk mixture into egg mixture.

Serves 6.

■ Custards can be made 3 days ahead.
■ Storage: Covered, in refrigerator.
■ Freeze: Not suitable.
■ Microwave: Pasta suitable.

MANGO ORANGE CREAMS WITH PASSION FRUIT SYRUP

1 cup fresh orange juice
3 cups water
18 extra large pasta shells
1 large mango, finely chopped
½lb ricotta cheese
3 tablespoons superfine sugar

PASSION FRUIT SYRUP
⅓ cup fresh passion fruit pulp
½ cup sugar
1 cup water

CHOCOLATE PASTA TENDRILS WITH RASPBERRY SAUCE

1 cup all-purpose flour
2 eggs, lightly beaten
2 squares (2oz) dark chocolate, melted
3 tablespoons unsweetened cocoa powder
1 tablespoon confectioners' sugar

RASPBERRY SAUCE
3 cups (¾lb) fresh or frozen raspberries
⅓ cup superfine sugar
⅓ cup water

Process flour, eggs, chocolate, cocoa powder and confectioners' sugar until mixture forms a ball. Knead dough on lightly floured surface for 10 minutes. Roll dough until ¹⁄₁₆ inch thick using pasta machine. Cut into ¹⁄₁₆ inch strips using pasta machine.

Add pasta to large pan of boiling water, boil, uncovered, about 3 minutes or until just tender; drain. Rinse pasta under cold water; drain. Serve pasta with raspberry sauce and extra raspberries, if desired.

Raspberry Sauce: Combine all ingredients in pan, stir over heat until sugar is dissolved. Cook, uncovered, about 3 minutes or until berries are soft. Push mixture through sieve to remove seeds; cover, refrigerate until cold.

Serves 4.

■ Pasta and sauce can be made a day ahead.
■ Storage: Covered, in refrigerator.
■ Freeze: Sauce suitable.
■ Microwave: Pasta suitable.

LEFT: From left: Mango Orange Creams with Passion Fruit Syrup, Caramel Cream Custards.
BELOW: Chocolate Pasta Tendrils with Raspberry Sauce.

Bring fresh orange juice and water to boil in pan, add pasta, boil, uncovered, until pasta is just tender; drain; cool.

Combine mango, cheese and sugar in bowl; mix well. Fill pasta shells with mango mixture. Serve shells with passion fruit syrup.

Passion Fruit Syrup: Combine all ingredients in pan, stir over heat until sugar is dissolved. Bring to boil, simmer, uncovered, 5 minutes or until slightly thickened; cool.

Serves 6.

■ Filling and syrup can be made a day ahead.
■ Storage: Covered, in refrigerator.
■ Freeze: Not suitable.
■ Microwave: Pasta suitable.

MERINGUE-TOPPED CITRUS ORZO PUDDING

⅔ cup orzo pasta
1½ cups milk
1 teaspoon grated lemon zest
1 teaspoon grated orange zest
¼ cup finely chopped glace apricots
½ cup sour cream
4 egg yolks
¼ cup cornstarch
½ cup superfine sugar
¼ cup lemon juice
¼ cup fresh orange juice
1 cup milk, extra

MERINGUE TOPPING
4 egg whites
⅓ cup superfine sugar
3 tablespoons slivered
   almonds, toasted
1 tablespoon dried currants

Combine pasta, milk and zest in pan, stir until boiling. Simmer, covered, about 10 minutes or until pasta is tender and mixture is thick; stir several times during cooking. Remove from heat, stir in apricots and sour cream; cool.

Beat egg yolks, cornstarch and sugar to a paste in pan, stir in juices and extra milk, stir mixture over heat until custard boils and thickens. Stir custard into pasta mixture. Spread mixture over base of deep ovenproof dish (4 cup capacity).

Just before serving, spread custard mixture with topping. Bake in 350°F oven about 5 minutes or until topping is lightly browned. Serve hot.

Meringue Topping: Beat egg whites in small bowl with electric mixer until soft peaks form, gradually add sugar, beating until dissolved between each addition. Fold in almonds and currants.

Serves 6.

■ Recipe can be prepared a day ahead.
■ Storage: Covered, in refrigerator.
■ Freeze: Not suitable.
■ Microwave: Not suitable.

FETTUCCINE WITH APPLE BUTTERSCOTCH SAUCE

3 cups apple juice
5oz fettuccine pasta

APPLE BUTTERSCOTCH SAUCE
2 large apples, peeled
2 tablespoons sugar
¼ cup water
¼ teaspoon ground cinnamon
¼ cup (½ stick) butter
⅔ cup firmly packed dark
   brown sugar
½ cup whipping cream
1 teaspoon rum

Bring juice to boil in pan, add pasta, boil, uncovered, until just tender; drain. Serve hot sauce over hot pasta.

Apple Butterscotch Sauce: Slice apples thinly, combine in pan with sugar, water and cinnamon, simmer, covered, about 10 minutes or until tender; drain.

Melt butter in pan, add dark brown sugar and cream, stir until combined. Simmer, uncovered, without stirring, 5 minutes. Remove from heat, stir in rum and apples.

Serves 4.

■ Recipe can be made 3 hours ahead.
■ Storage: Covered, at room temperature.
■ Freeze: Not suitable.
■ Microwave: Pasta suitable.

APRICOT NOODLE CREAM

½lb twisted spaghetti pasta
1⅔ cups (½lb) chopped
   dried apricots
4 eggs, lightly beaten
1 cup heavy cream
½ cup milk
½ cup superfine sugar
½ teaspoon ground nutmeg
½ teaspoon ground cinnamon
½ teaspoon superfine sugar, extra

Add pasta to large pan of boiling water, boil, uncovered, until just tender, drain; cool. Soak apricots in boiling water 5 minutes, drain; cool.

Combine eggs, cream, milk, sugar and half each of the nutmeg and cinnamon in bowl, stir in pasta and apricots. Pour mixture into a shallow ovenproof dish (4 cup capacity). Combine remaining nutmeg and cinnamon with extra sugar, sprinkle over pasta mixture.

Place dish in roasting pan, pour enough boiling water into pan to come halfway up sides of dish. Bake in 350°F oven about 40 minutes or until just set.

Serves 4.

■ Recipe best made just before serving.
■ Freeze: Not suitable.
■ Microwave: Pasta suitable.

RIGHT: Clockwise from front: Fettuccine with Apple Butterscotch Sauce, Meringue-Topped Citrus Orzo Pudding, Apricot Noodle Cream.

HOW TO MAKE FRESH PASTA

Step-by-Step Guide

With our easy instructions and pictures, you can soon learn to make fresh pasta by hand or machine; use quantities of plain or flavored pasta dough as specified in individual recipes. We also give more details on how to cook pasta (including how to microwave it), and how to reheat it correctly.

Here are recipes for plain pasta dough and the flavor variations we used in this book:

PLAIN PASTA

**2 cups all-purpose flour
3 eggs**

HAND METHOD

1. Sift flour onto bench or into bowl, make well in center, add eggs to well. Using fingers, gradually mix flour into eggs.

2. Press mixture into a ball.

3. Knead dough for about 10 minutes or until smooth and elastic. Cover dough, stand 20 minutes.

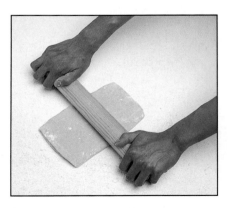

4. Roll dough on lightly floured surface to desired thickness.

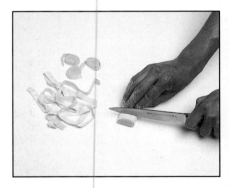

5. To make fettuccine or tagliatelle pasta, roll sheets of pasta dough firmly. Cut roll into slices, unroll slices into strips.

MACHINE METHOD

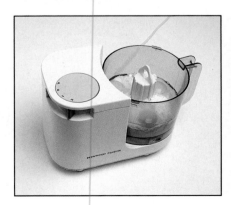

1. Combine ingredients in food processor.

2. Process ingredients until mixture forms a ball.

3. Knead dough on lightly floured surface until smooth. Cut dough in half, roll each half through pasta machine set on thickest setting. Fold dough in half, roll through machine. Repeat folding and rolling several times until dough is very smooth and elastic, dusting dough with a little extra flour, when necessary.

4. Roll dough through machine, adjusting setting to become less thick with each roll, dusting dough with a little extra flour, when necessary. Roll to desired thickness.

5. To make fettuccine, roll dough through fettuccine attachment of machine, dusting dough with a little extra flour, when necessary.

WHOLE-WHEAT PASTA

1¼ cups all-purpose flour
¾ cup whole-wheat flour
3 eggs

Make as for plain pasta dough.

CHILI PASTA

2 cups all-purpose flour
1 teaspoon chili powder
3 eggs

Make as for plain pasta dough, combining chili powder with flour.

SPINACH PASTA

¼ cup chopped cooked spinach
2½ cups all-purpose flour
2 eggs

Squeeze excess moisture from spinach, add to flour with eggs. Continue as for plain pasta dough.

PEPPER PASTA

2 cups all-purpose flour
1½ teaspoons seasoned pepper
1 teaspoon paprika
3 eggs

Make as for plain pasta dough, combining pepper and paprika with flour.

HERBED PASTA

2 cups all-purpose flour
¼ cup chopped fresh basil
3 eggs

Make as for plain pasta dough, adding basil with eggs.

TOMATO PASTA

1¾ cups all-purpose flour
2½oz package dry tomato soup mix
3 eggs

Make as for plain pasta dough, combining soup mix with flour.

TO MAKE RAVIOLI

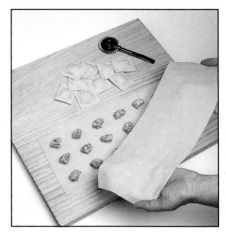

Roll pasta dough as specified in individual recipes, place filling at even intervals over dough. Brush lightly between filling and along edges with water. Top with a sheet of pasta, press firmly between filling and along edges. Cut into ravioli shapes using a pastry wheel; follow size indicated in individual recipes. Cook as specified in individual recipes.

TO MAKE TORTELLINI

Roll pasta dough to desired thickness, cut into rounds following size indicated in individual recipes. Top rounds with filling, lightly brush edges of rounds with water, fold rounds in half, press edges together to seal. Fold edges up, press corners together firmly. Cook as specified in individual recipes.

121

PASTA FACTS

Many nations claim to have invented macaroni (the generic term for all shapes and flavors of pasta) but it is in Italy that pasta-making was perfected. As a result, most of the macaronis bear Italian names. When these names are translated, they describe the shape or type of pasta, for example: lasagne means "broad-leafed".

Macaroni products can be divided into four basic groups — cords, tubes, ribbons, and special shapes such as shells, crests, etc. There is a wide range of sizes and shapes within each group. Ravioli and tortellini are small shapes with fillings of cheese, vegetables, beef, pork, chicken, etc.

Pasta can be fresh or dried; one can be substituted for the other. Use the same weight as specified for dried or fresh when substituting.

The noodles we used are mostly of Oriental origin; these are available in different types and sizes, including wonton skins. A big difference between pasta and noodles is the type of recipes they are used in. We used noodles mostly in recipes with an Asian influence, although occasionally we used wonton skins, etc., as a convenient pastry for ravioli.

TO COOK PASTA

Cook all forms of pasta in plenty of boiling water. Use a large saucepan or small boiler. Three-quarters fill the pan with hot water, cover, place over high heat, bring water to a fast rolling boil, add sprinkling of salt, if desired. Add pasta gradually, so water does not go off the boil.

When cooking spaghetti, vermicelli or any of the "long goods", as they are called, hold long strands at one end, place other ends in the boiling water. The pasta will begin to soften in the hot water and it is then simple to lower strands into saucepan, coiling them neatly inside pan.

Check individual recipes or instructions on packet for cooking times. Cooking time of pasta varies according to individual manufacturers; freshness of the product, too, will affect cooking time (home-made pasta cooks much more quickly than the commercial product). Pasta should not be overcooked; it should be "al dente" (to the tooth) – tender but firm.

TO MICROWAVE PASTA

You can microwave fresh and dried pasta successfully, though each takes about the same time as in conventional cooking.

Place pasta in large microwave proof bowl, pour in enough boiling water to cover pasta generously. Microwave, covered, on HIGH (100% power), until pasta is just tender; drain. Take care not to overcook pasta.

TO REHEAT PASTA

Place pasta in heatproof bowl, add enough boiling water to cover pasta, stand for I minute; drain well.

TO REHEAT PASTA IN A MICROWAVE OVEN

Place pasta in microwave proof bowl, cover, microwave on HIGH (100% power) for 1 minute at a time, stirring occasionally, or until heated through; drain well.

Glossary

Here are some terms, names and
alternatives to help everyone use and understand our recipes perfectly.

ALCOHOL: is optional but gives special flavor. You can use fruit juice or water instead to make up the liquid content in our recipes.
ALMONDS
Ground: we used commercially ground packaged almonds.
Sliced: almonds cut into thin slices.
Slivered: almonds cut into slivers.
ARROWROOT: used mostly for thickening. Cornstarch can be used instead.
BACON SLICES: we used thick slices where specified.
BEAN SPROUTS: we used mung bean sprouts; these should be topped and tailed; available fresh or canned in brine.

BEANS, BLACK: are fermented, salted soya beans. Canned and dried black beans can be substituted. Drain and rinse canned variety, soak and rinse dried variety. Leftover beans will keep for months in an airtight container in the refrigerator. Mash beans when cooking to release flavor.
BEEF
Chuck: is cut from the neck of the animal. Flesh is firm, with coarse grain, red color and little fat. Long cooking is recommended.
BELL PEPPERS: capsicums.
BOUILLON CUBES: available in beef, chicken or vegetable flavors. Use 1 large crumbled stock cube to every 2 cups water. These cubes contain salt, so allow for this when seasoning food.

From left: Red bell pepper, pimientos.

BREAD CRUMBS
Fresh: use 1- or 2-day-old white breadmade into crumbs by grating, blending or processing.

Unseasoned packaged: use fine packaged unseasoned bread crumbs.
BROCCOLI, CHINESE (gai lum): remove and discard fibrous parts of the stem, cut flowerets away from stems and leaves. If using remaining stems, peel away any tough skin with peeler and chop stems.

Chinese broccoli.

BUTTER: use salted or unsalted (sweet) butter.
BUTTERMILK: is now made by adding a culture to skim milk to give a slightly acid flavor; skim milk can be substituted if preferred.
CABANOSSI: a type of sausage; also known as cabana.

From top: Chorizo sausage, cabanossi.

CABBAGE: large leafy vegetable available in several different varieties.
Chinese: also known as Nappa cabbage.

Clockwise from top: Red cabbage, Chinese cabbage, savoy cabbage.

CARAMEL TOPPING: a caramel-flavored syrup usually used in milk drinks or on pancakes and ice cream.
CHEESE
Bocconcini: small balls of mild, delicate cheese packaged in water or whey to keep them white and soft. The water should be just milky and cheese should be white; yellowing indicates that it is stale.

Cheddar: we used a full-flavored firm cheddar.
Cream cheese: unripened, smooth, spreadable cheese.
Cottage: soft, unripened, mild-tasting curd cheese of different fat content from skim milk to full-cream milk.
Fresh goats' milk: we used a mild-flavored goats' cheese.
Gruyere: a Swiss cheese with small holes and a nutty, slightly salty flavor.
Jarlsberg: a Norwegian cheese made from cows' milk; it has large holes and a mild nutty taste.
Kefalogravier: a semi-hard cheese with a smooth texture and a mild salty after-taste; made from sheep's milk.
Mozzarella: a fresh, semi-soft cheese with a delicate, clean, fresh curd taste; has a low melting point and stringy texture when heated.
Neufchatel: soft, unripened or fresh curd cheese. It resembles cream cheese but contains more moisture.
Parmesan: sharp-tasting cheese used as a flavor accent. We prefer to use fresh Parmesan cheese, however, it is available already finely grated.
Pecorino: hard cheese, straw-colored with grainy texture and sharp-tangy flavor.
Ricotta: a fresh, unripened, light curd cheese of rich flavor.
True blue: a smooth and creamy white-blue mold cheese.
CHILIES: are available in many different types and sizes. The small ones (bird's eye or bird peppers) are the hottest. Use tight rubber gloves when chopping fresh chilies as they can burn your skin. The seeds are the hottest part of the chilies so remove them if you want to reduce the heat content of recipes.
Chili powder: ground dried chilies.
Chili sauce: we used a hot or sweet Chinese variety. It consists of chilies, salt and vinegar. We use it sparingly so that you can easily increase amounts in recipes to suit your taste.
Dried chili flakes: are available at Asian food stores.
CHORIZO SAUSAGE: Spanish and Mexican highly spiced pork sausages seasoned with garlic, cayenne pepper, chili, etc. They are ready to eat when bought. If unavailable, use a spicy salami. See picture with cabanossi.
CHICORY: a curly-leafed vegetable, mainly used in salads.

Chicory.

CILANTRO: also known as coriander and Chinese parsley, it is available fresh. The leaves, roots and stems can be used.

Clockwise from right: Cilantro, ground coriander, flat-leafed parsley.

CREAM
Half-and-Half: thin pouring cream.
Heavy: use when specified in recipes.
Light Sour: a less dense commercially cultured soured cream; do not substitute this for sour cream.
Whipping: is specified when necessary in recipes.
Reduced: a canned product with 25 percent fat content.
Sour: a thick commercially cultured soured cream.
CREME DE CACAO: chocolate-flavored liqueur.
CURRY POWDER: a convenient combination of spices in powdered form. Curry powder consists of chili, coriander, cumin, fennel, fenugreek and turmeric in varying proportions.
CUSTARD POWDER: pudding mix.
DILL PICKLE: pickled baby cucumber.
DUCK, CHINESE ROAST: available from Asian food stores.
DUCK LIVER PATE: use chicken liver pate if unavailable.
FENNEL: vegetable with aniseed-tasting bulb and leaves; bulb can be eaten uncooked in salads or may be braised, steamed or stir-fried in savory dishes. Leaves can be chopped and added to dishes.
FISH SAUCE: an essential ingredient in the cooking of a number of South East Asian countries, including Thailand and Vietnam. It is made from the liquid drained from salted, fermented anchovies. It has a very strong smell and taste. Use sparingly until you acquire the taste.
FIVE-SPICE POWDER: a pungent mixture of ground spices which includes cinnamon, cloves, fennel, star anise and Szechuan peppers.
GARBANZO BEANS: canned chick peas. They are a staple food in the Middle East; are available from supermarkets and health food shops.
GARAM MASALA: there are many variations of the combinations of cardamom, cinnamon, cloves, coriander, cumin and nutmeg used to make up this spice, used often in Indian cooking. Sometimes pepper is used to make a hot

variation. Garam masala is readily available in jars.

GARLIC: strong-scented pungent bulb with a distinctive taste. A bulb consists of cloves; use number of cloves specified in individual recipes. See picture with red onions.

GINGERROOT:

Fresh or green: scrape away outside skin and grate, chop or slice gingerroot as required. Fresh, peeled gingerroot can be preserved with enough dry sherry to cover; keep in jar in refrigerator; it will keep for months.

Ground: is also available but should not be substituted for fresh gingerroot.

Fresh gingerroot.

GRAND MARNIER: an orange-flavored liqueur. Cointreau can be substituted.

HERBS: we have specified when to use fresh or dried herbs. We used dried (not ground) herbs in the proportion of 1:4 for fresh herbs; for example, 1 teaspoon dried herbs instead of 4 teaspoons chopped fresh herbs.

HOISIN SAUCE: a thick, sweet Chinese barbeque sauce made from salted black beans, onions and garlic.

HORSERADISH CREAM: paste of horseradish, oil, mustard and flavorings.

JAM: conserve.

KAHLUA: a Mexican liqueur flavored with coffee.

KIRSCH: a liqueur distilled from cherries.

KIWIFRUIT: Chinese gooseberries.

LASAGNE, INSTANT: these pasta sheets don't need to be pre-cooked; check package directions; available from supermarkets.

LEMON GRASS: needs to be bruised or chopped before using. It will keep in a jug of water at room temperature for several weeks; the water must be changed daily. It can be bought dried. To reconstitute: place several pieces of dried lemon grass in a bowl; cover with hot water, stand 20 minutes; drain. This amount is a substitute for 1 stalk of fresh lemon grass.

Lemon grass.

LOBSTER: crayfish.

MALIBU: tropical coconut drink flavored with light Jamaican rum liqueur.

MARINARA MIX: a mixture of uncooked, chopped seafood usually including shrimp, mussels, fish and octopus or squid.

MARZIPAN: a paste made from marzipan meal.

MIRIN: a sweet rice wine used in Japanese cooking. Substitute 1 teaspoon sugar and 1 teaspoon dry sherry for 4 teaspoons of mirin, if preferred.

MIXED SPICE: a blend of ground spices usually consisting of cinnamon, all-spice and nutmeg.

MUSHROOMS: We used fresh mushrooms, plus other different types of mushrooms in our recipes.

Clockwise from left: Oyster mushrooms, shitake mushrooms, Chinese dried mushrooms.

MUSSEL MEAT: cooked mussels removed from the shell. See picture with sea scallops.

MUSTARD, SEEDED: a French style of mustard with crushed mustard seeds.

MUSTARD SEEDS: tiny seeds used in curries, pickling and making mustard; seeds can be black, (spicy and piquant), brown (less piquant) or white (milder).

NOODLES: see picture below.

OIL: polyunsaturated vegetable oil.

Olive: we used a virgin olive oil but use the grade you prefer. Olive oil comes in several different grades with each grade having a different flavor. The most flavorsome is the extra virgin variety usually used in homemade dressings. Extra virgin olive oil is the purest quality virgin oil. Virgin oil is obtained only from the pulp of high-grade fruit. Pure olive oil is pressed from the pulp and kernels of second grade olives. Extra light olive oil is lighter in color and flavor to pure and virgin.

Oriental Sesame: made from roasted, crushed white sesame seeds. It is always used in small quantities. Do not use for frying.

ONION, RED: red-skinned, pink-fleshed variety, almost odorless and popular in salads.

ONION, GREEN: also known as spring onion or scallion. See picture below.

From left: Garlic, bulb and cloves, green onions, red onion.

OYSTER-FLAVORED SAUCE: a rich brown sauce made from oysters cooked in salt and soy sauce, then thickened with

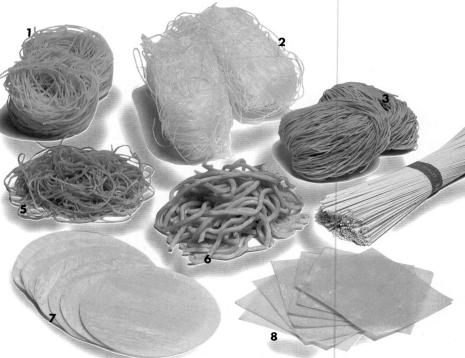

Noodles used in this book: 1. Capellini egg noodles. 2. rice vermicelli, 3. dried egg noodles, 4. Japanese somen noodles, 5. fine fresh egg noodles, 6. fresh egg noodles, 7. gow gees pastry, 8. egg pastry sheets.

different types of starches.

PANCETTA: is Italian in origin; is a ready-to-eat processed meat made from pork belly which has been salted, cured and lightly spiced. See picture with pastrami.

PARSLEY, FLAT-LEAFED: popular herb also known as continental or Italian parsley. See picture with cilantro.

PASTA: See picture below.

Lasagnette: wide strips of pasta with curled edges. Also known as papardelle pasta.

Paglia e fieno: packaged combination of spinach and plain fettuccine. Use plain or spinach if unavailable.

PASTA SAUCE: we used bottled products; one containing beef and one without meat, based on tomatoes; available from supermarkets.

PASTRAMI: highly seasoned smoked beef ready to eat when bought.

Clockwise from top: Prosciutto, pastrami, pancetta.

PASTRY, READY ROLLED PUFF: frozen sheets of puff pastry available from supermarkets.

PEAS

Snow: also known as Chinese pea pods.

Sugar snap: a young tender spring pea with edible pod.

From left: Snow peas, sugar snap peas.

PECANS: nuts of the hickory tree with a sweet, oily kernel; walnuts can be substituted.

PEPPERCORNS, GREEN: berries of the pepper plant; available in cans or bottles from supermarkets.

PEPPER, SEASONED: a combination of pepper, red bell pepper, garlic flakes, paprika and natural chicken extract.

PIMIENTOS (sweet red peppers): are preserved in brine in cans or jars. See picture with bell peppers.

PLUM SAUCE: a dipping sauce which consists of plums preserved in vinegar, sweetened with sugar and flavored with chilies and spices.

PORK, BARBEQUED RED: roasted pork fillets available from many Asian food and specialty stores.

PORT WINE JELLY: a port-flavored jelly preserve; apple jelly can be substituted.

PROSCIUTTO: uncooked, unsmoked ham cured in salt, ready to eat when bought. See picture with pastrami.

ROCK CORNISH HEN: small bird about ¾lb to 1lb.

RUM: we used a dark underproof rum.

SAFFRON: the most expensive of all spices, is available in threads or ground form. It is made from the dried stamens of the crocus flower.

SAKE: Japan's favorite rice wine; is used in cooking, marinading and as part of dipping sauces. If sake is unavailable, dry sherry, vermouth or brandy can be substituted.

SALMON: we used a farmed variety of salmon available all year.

SALMON ROE: caviar, eggs of salmon.

SAMBAL OELEK: a paste made from ground chilies and salt.

SEA SCALLOPS: we used sea scallops with the orange coral attached; they require minimal preparation.

From top: Sea scallops, mussel meat.

SHRIMP PASTE: a powerful dark brown flavoring made from salted dried shrimp.

SNOW PEA SPROUTS: young shoots from sprouted snow peas.

SOY SAUCE: made from fermented soya beans. The light sauce is generally used with white meat, the darker variety with red meat. There is a multi-purpose salt-reduced sauce available, also Japanese soy sauce. It is a matter of personal taste which sauce you use.

SPINACH: a soft-leaved vegetable, more delicate in taste than Swiss chard; however, young Swiss chard can be substituted.

From left: Spinach, Swiss chard.

Picture shows some of the pastas used in this book: 1. angels' hair pasta, 2. extra large pasta shells, 3. radiatore pasta, 4. whole-wheat pasta wheels, 5. small macaroni pasta, 6. linguine pasta, 7. vegetable pasta twists, 8. pasta crests.

SUGAR
Brown: we used dark or light as specified.
Confectioners': powdered sugar.
Superfine: fine granulated table sugar.
SWISS CHARD: remove coarse white stems, cook green leafy parts as individual recipes indicate. See picture on page 125.
TERIYAKI MARINADE: a blend of soy sauce, wine, vinegar and spices.
TOAST BREAD: thick sliced white bread.
TOFU: made from boiled, crushed soy beans to give a type of milk, a coagulant is added, then the curds are drained and cotton tofu is the result; this is the ordinary firm tofu used in this book. Silken tofu is undrained and more fragile. Store tofu in the refrigerator covered with water, which must be changed daily.
TOMATO
Ketchup: we used tomato ketchup.
Paste: a concentrated tomato puree used in flavoring soups, stews, sauces, etc.
Puree: canned, pureed tomatoes (not tomato paste). Use fresh, peeled, pureed tomatoes as a substitute, if preferred.
Sun-dried: are dried tomatoes sometimes bottled in oil.
Supreme: a canned product consisting of tomatoes, onions, celery, bell peppers and seasonings.
TURKEY BREAST ROLL: ready-to-eat turkey available from delicatessens.
VECON PASTE: a natural vegetable bouillon paste available in health food stores.
VINEGAR: we used both white and brown (malt) vinegar in this book.
Balsamic: originated in the province of Modena, Italy. Regional wine is specially processed then aged in antique wooden casks to give pungent flavor.
Cider: vinegar made from fermented apples.
Red wine: made from red wine, often flavored with herbs, spices, fruit, etc.
Rice: a colorless seasoned vinegar containing sugar and salt.
WASABI PASTE: a paste made from Japanese horseradish; available from Asian food stores.
WINE: we used good-quality dry white and red wines.
Green ginger: an Australian-made alcoholic sweet wine infused with finely ground gingerroot.
WONTON SKINS: are thin squares or rounds of fresh noodle dough. Use egg pastry sheets if unavailable; available from Asian food stores.
WORCESTERSHIRE SAUCE: is a spicy sauce used mainly on red meat.
ZEST: colored skin of citrus fruit.

Index

CUP & SPOON MEASUREMENTS

To ensure accuracy in your recipes use standard measuring equipment.
a) 8 fluid oz cup for measuring liquids.
b) a graduated set of four cups – measuring 1 cup, half, third and quarter cup – for items such as flour, sugar, etc.
When measuring in these fractional cups level off at the brim.
c) a graduated set of five spoons: tablespoon (½ fluid oz liquid capacity), teaspoon, half, quarter and eighth teaspoons.
All spoon measurements are level.
We have used large eggs with an average weight of 2oz each in all our recipes.

Home Library
Salads
Sensational recipes for all occasions

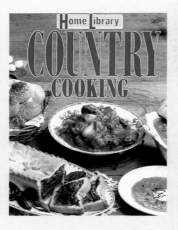

Home Library
COUNTRY COOKING

Home Library
Healthy Heart Cookbook
LOWER CHOLESTEROL

Home Library
VEGETARIAN COOKING

THE BEST **Home Library**
SEAFOOD RECIPES

Home Library
Italian
COOKING CLASS COOKBOOK

Home Library
CHICKEN COOKBOOK
PLUS duck, quail, turkey, goose and more

Home Library
PASTA COOKBOOK
More than 170 recipes

Home Library
CHINESE COOKING CLASS COOKBOOK

Home Library
STARTERS AND SOUPS

Home Library
BEGINNERS' COOKBOOK

Home Library
FINGER FOOD
Best ever party food
Tempting hot and cold savouries
Do ahead and freezing tips